GW00361471

VELOCETTE
FLAT-TWINS

OSPREY
COLLECTOR'S
LIBRARY

VELOCETTE
FLAT-TWINS

**All flat twins from LE of
1948—plus LE MkII, Vogue,
Valiant, Vee Line and
Viceroy—to LE MkIII of 1971**

Roy Bacon

Published in 1985 by Osprey Publishing Limited
12–14 Long Acre, London WC2E 9LP
Member company of the George Philip Group

British Library Cataloguing in Publication Data
Bacon, Roy H.
    Velocette: the flat twins: all flat twins from LE
    of 1948—plus LE MK II, Vogue, Valiant, Vee
    Line and Viceroy—to LE MK III of 1971.—
    (Osprey collector's library)
    1. Velocette motorcycle
    I. Title
    629.2'275   TL448.V4
ISBN 0-85045-632-O

Editor Tim Parker

Filmset and printed in England by
BAS Printers Limited, Over Wallop, Hampshire

Contents

Acknowledgements

I once said I would not do a book on Velocettes in the Collector's Series but maybe I meant not on the singles. For those one needs to have spent time with camshafts and clutches learning the lore. Mine was secondhand with the camshaft joys learnt watching a friend who removed the head and then trod happily on the kickstarter. Hunting teeth were explained to him.

The clutch lore I learnt in part from my old friend, gone but never forgotten, Fred Launchbury. He had a Mark VIII and involved me in removing the baked on R from the rear hub. He also showed me the trick of keeping clutch adjustment when push starting. You pull the lever and then tap the clutch with your toe to knock the plates apart.

So without real in-depth knowledge of the singles I steered clear but when a gap came in the programme, I felt could manage flat twins to fill it. With a few notes on the early days and the two vertical twins to round out the picture.

Help with the work came from arch Velo man Ivan Rhodes who put me in touch with Dennis Frost who is the historian and registrar of the LE Velo Club. Dennis most kindly went through my notes on the engine and frame numbers, added missing ones and checked and corrected my data on the changes and when they occurred.

If this was not enough he also put me in touch with Mr. B. Bennett who owns two of the Viceroy powered DMW Deemster models and who took the best scooter award at the 1983 Classic Bike Show at Belle Vue with one of them. Thanks to Mr. Bennett we have two pictures of this rare model. Dennis also put me in touch with Mike Payne who provided information on the hovercraft application of the Viceroy.

Most of the pictures and line drawings came from the EMAP archives which hold the old *Motor Cycle Weekly* files for which my thanks. Others were from the *MCN* files courtesy of Jim Lindsay and among the collection were some with the imprint of the professionals. Pictures from them included the work of James Brymer, Arthur Hind, Peter Lea and Donald Page.

As usual all the pictures were returned to their files after publication and I have tried to make contact to clear copyright. If my letter failed to reach you or I have used an unmarked print without realising this, please accept my apologies.

Finally, as always, my thanks to Tim Parker.

Roy Bacon
Niton, Isle of Wight
July 1985

1 | Starting with the famous singles

Any Velocette story is a family tale, for just one headed the firm from start to finish with father, son, second son and grandson at the handlebars in turn. The effect of this was to produce a series of machines that followed a pattern, partly in their design but more in the philosophy behind the design which was to remain steadfast for some 60 years.

The character of the marque came from the family who determined to build a product of value, one nice to own and use, and one that reflected quality in all its aspects. They always strove to achieve the right technical solution to any problem, not regardless of cost, but with cost kept in mind as a factor of value for money and not the paramount issue.

So Velocette features were well engineered, used good materials and were well made which made them desirable but expensive in comparison with their contemporaries. Of course they were usually much better than them as well but at times this made them too costly for many buyers no matter how desirable they were.

The effect of this policy was to produce machines of character that stood out from the ruck. They trod their own path with little aknowledgement to any passing styling trend but often were in the forefront of technical innovation and introduced a number of ideas which became idiosyncrasies of the marque and the subject of myths and legends which in time became part of the

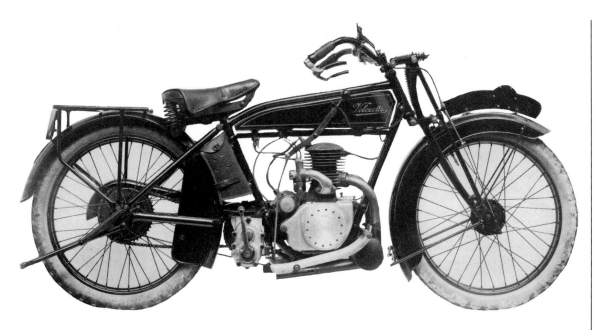

Velocette two-stroke from the early twenties with crude front fork but sophisticated engine oiling

folklore of the make. They all helped to build up a clientele of discerning and dedicated enthusiasts who remained loyal to the firm for life.

The family that achieved this originated from Germany where their name was Gutgemann and during the 19th century young Johannes moved to Birmingham and married. In later years he changed his name to John Goodman but before

then became involved in a variety of enterprises. These included pill making, rickshaws and bicycles and the last inevitably led him to early motorcycles.

His bicycle firm was named Taylor Gue and in 1905 built their first motorcycle which they called a Veloce. It was a prosaic 2 hp belt drive single and met with such little success that the firm went into liquidation later the same year.

Despite this, John Goodman, who used the name John Taylor during this period, started up a new firm using the Veloce name and it was this that was to remain in use for another 65 years. At first they made a variety of items but in 1910 returned to motorcycles with a model which had a 276 cc single cylinder engine built in unit with a two-speed gearbox. This had a mechanical oil pump so despite the belt drive to the rear wheel it was of an advanced design. Maybe too advanced for it did not sell well so Veloce introduced a straightforward 500 cc single with belt drive.

They also brought out a 2½ hp model in standard and ladies' model while by 1914 the 500 cc machine was joined by a version with a three-speed rear hub.

More important was a lightweight introduced in 1913 and such models were then referred to as motorcyclettes so the new machine had to become a Velocette. The name stuck and years later when the firm sought to introduce its 350 cc

camshaft model as a Veloce the dealers protested and the tank transfers were quickly changed.

The first Velocette was a two-stroke and contained features to remain in use for over a decade. The engine had a one piece iron head and barrel which sat above an overhung crankshaft in a crankcase with a detachable door on the right. On the left went a large flywheel and inboard of it the belt drive to the rear wheel and chain drive to the magneto tucked away behind the cylinder out of harm.

Two points in particular showed the firm's determination to do the job correctly regardless of convention. The first concerned engine lubrication for at a time when petroil was the normal choice the Goodmans, father and sons, chose an

Characteristic outside flywheel of mid-1920s 250 cc two-stroke single. Typical Velo clutch

automatic system to supply the big end via a regulating valve the rider could adjust. The family considered lubrication important and mixing fuel and oil messy.

The second point concerned the engine placing. Convention put the cylinder on the machine centre line with the rear wheel pulley set out as needed to align with the front one. Rather than do this and accept the increased bearing loads that resulted the Goodmans placed the belt as close as possible to the tyre. The engine, well that they just moved over so it hung out on the right side of the frame.

The original model was quickly joined by one

Bottom **An early KTT with coil valve springs for its 350 cc ohc engine**

Below **The last of the early series of two strokes with overhung crankshaft in 1929**

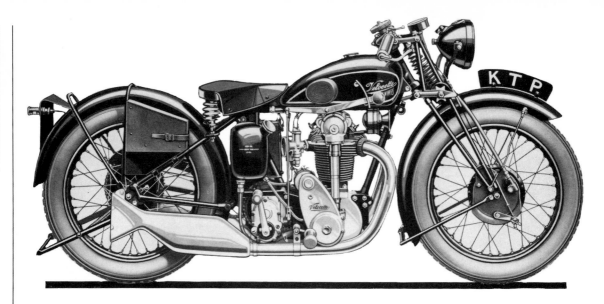

'Kut price' K model with coil ignition, dynamo in magneto's home and points on camshaft end, built 1930–31

with a two-speed gearbox, without clutch, and this had all chain drive with the primary inboard of the final. This arrangement suited the engine position and continued after the First World War along with a three-speed version although this still lacked a clutch.

It was 1922 before the firm decided to add a clutch and to keep to their existing machine layout the Goodmans had to fit this in behind the final drive sprocket. The alternative would have been conventional but with the engine sprocket greatly hung out from the crankshaft or with the whole engine moved over in the frame. The first was bad engineering and the second bad commerce so the famous thin Velocette clutch was born. It and its derivatives were to live for half a century and create much Velocette folklore.

The two-stroke model continued on to 1926 in a number of forms and while these were mainly quality products rather than utilitarian there were cheaper versions built. Often these seemed to be aimed at 'Mr Everyman' or 'the man in the street', two popular figures that crop up quite often in the history of motorcycling. It was said that if you could find the right key they

would unlock their wallets by the thousand to become mobile. It was an elusive dream that drove many companies to the wall and was to give Velocette problems over the years.

After missing a year the two-stroke continued as the model U up to 1929 but was then replaced by the GTP. This had a conventional built-up crankshaft but kept the outside flywheel on the left. An oil pump and contact breaker went on the right and a year or so later the pump was linked to the throttle so its output varied with that control. The GTP was a popular machine and remained in production up to the Second World War with a small batch being made for export just after it.

Velocette were not to build another two-stroke motorcycle until late 1960 and this had a number of interesting features as well as being lubricated by petroil. Long before that episode the firm had become known worldwide as makers of high quality singles with better than average performance. All had the Velocette

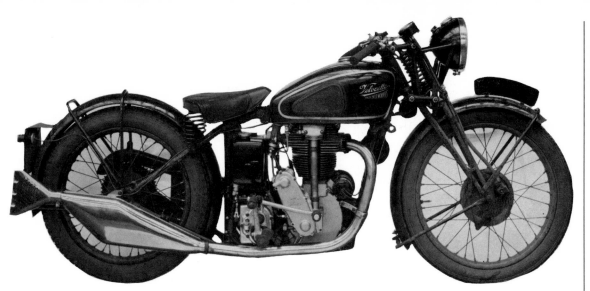

Much nicer—the KSS in 1936 and typical camshaft Velo

clutch, all had performance and all behaved in a way to attract the connoisseur.

Two strings of singles were built, these being the K series with an overhead camshaft and the M series which kept the valves upstairs but moved them with pushrods. The first camshaft machine was built in 1924 and set the format for the series. Narrow crankcase with the primary drive tucked well in to keep the bearing loads down. Thus the mains in a Velocette always looked small but were quite adequate for the loads they carried.

On the right a vertical shaft and bevels drove the camshaft and in production a hunting tooth design kept the loads from hammering one tooth all the time. Not all owners were to appreciate the quirks of such an arrangement but they learnt in time. The magneto went behind the cylinder where it was chain driven from the bottom bevel box and below this in the crankcase went a double gear pump. This was for the dry sump system adopted after problems with the initial layout.

It was a classic design and continued in various forms up to 1950. Prefixes were many and all began with the letter K with KSS and KTT being

perhaps the best known. There were lots more but all were of 350 cc.

The K series was very respected and commercially successful but in the hard times of the 1930s it was outside the price range of many. For those who could not manage to run to a KSS but needed more power than the GTP offered, Velocette designed the first of their M series, the MOV. This 250 cc machine came in 1933 and had the camshaft set high in the timing chest to keep the pushrod length down. It set a style that continued with the firm to the end of their days.

It was soon joined by a 350 cc version, the MAC, achieved by lengthening the stroke and later this was bored out to give the 500 cc MSS. All three models were popular and helped the fortunes of the firm for a good few years. The 350 and 500 cc models continued in production for many years, the larger model to the end, and the essence of the machines never changed, nor did the line of the engine.

Above **1937 example of the pushrod Velocette built as MOV, MAC and MSS models in 250, 350 and 500 cc**

Below **The 1939 Mark VIII KTT with its air suspension at the rear. A very good engine**

The Roarer with Stanley Woods aboard

Velocette got the K model off the ground with success in the TT but behind that lay a deal of hard work and some sound engineering. One of the early problems lay in the valve gear and to investigate this a stroboscope was brought from London. Using this it was soon realized that for once the rockers were trying to follow the cam-shaft. In an ohv engine the valve gear floated under racing conditions and cam forms had been arrived at empirically to give the best power. Transferred to an ohc layout they either killed the performance or broke the valve gear.

The strobe also allowed the team to watch the crankcase walls flex and cylinder barrels move about but intelligent interpretation soon had the parts under control.

Alec Bennett won the 1926 Junior TT by over ten minutes and won again in 1928 with Harold Willis second as he had been in 1927. Willis was an active motorcyclist and a unique character who became a director of the company and is remembered as much for his apt descriptive phrases as for his clever and innovative designs.

The best known and most copied of the latter was the positive stop foot gearchange which was introduced in 1928 and in time taken up by all manufacturers. He also tried a dualset and his name for it, 'Loch Ness Monster,' was both accurate and typical of the man. An early spring frame racer was called 'Spring-Heeled Jack,' and a blown single 'Whiffling Clara'. When this engine burnt its piston crown the damage was by mice while valves were nails and the camshaft engine a single knocker with twin cam jobs called double knockers. Sadly Willis died in 1939 and Velocette lost one of their best men.

Not that the firm was not led by people who knew their machines. They rode them and so did many of their staff so all Velocettes were rider's machines. The layout, set by the 1913 belt drive called for a slim engine with the weight all tucked in near the centre line of the machine. Furthermore the heavier items went under a line drawn through the wheel centres and this always helped to give a machine ease of handling.

For many the narrow lines of the Velocette enabled it to be built light and slim while its rivals fattened and put on weight. Handling is a special subject, part art and part science but it is worth remembering that many years later certain good handling twins became less so when they grew heavy alternators and triplex primary chains well set out from the tyre line. Moving the wheels over cured the problem so maybe by chance Velocette came onto a magic formula. Fortunately for those that care about such matters they stuck to it and incorporated it into their design principles.

Thus Velocette came to the late 1930s. They had won their third Junior TT courtesy of Freddie Hicks but from then on the pickings in the Isle of Man had been lean. For all that just off the

The Velocette stands at Earls Court in November 1954 all ready for the public

日本に来た名車たち　*The John Bull Motor Cycles*

ベロセット 1962年　LE　マークⅢ

351 DLH

top placings came many a KTT in private hands and this model built up a fine reputation everywhere it was raced.

The works team also ran a 500 cc machine and in the Senior TT this was third in 1934 ridden by Walter Rusk and second in 1936 under Stanley Woods who repeated this performance the following year. He managed to make it three in a row in 1938 but of more importance to the firm that year was his victory in the Junior TT. He won that event again in 1939 and postwar there were more victories for Bob Foster in 1947 and Freddie Frith in 1948 and 1949.

Frith won the 350 cc World Championship that year winning all five races and Foster took the 1950 title but Velocette had been successful in championships before then. The predecessor of the World title had been the European one introduced in 1938 and for that year and 1939 Velocette took the 350 cc class with Ted Mellors the rider.

Well before then it became all too clear that an unblown single was no longer competitive as

BMW, Gilera, Guzzi and DKW showed what could be done with blown multis. To meet this challenge Velocette decided to build a new machine and settled on two cylinders as they felt a four to be too complex for the hurly-burly of the Continental Circus while their experience with Clara had put them off blown singles.

At the same time they needed a twin cylinder road model to compete with the 1938 Triumph which had proved very successful. Due to the war no other firm was to get a vertical twin into production until the conflict was over and then the one major firm without one was to be Velocette.

They decided that roadster and racer should be based on the same principles which did not include the parallel twin layout as used by Triumph. This vibrated so would not do while a flat twin as used by BMW was too wide. However, the German design was fast despite its frontal area and with shaft drive kept clean and oil free, an important factor in racing tyre life.

The snag was the handling and many were the tales surrounding the effects of shaft drive and an in-line crankshaft on this area. Of the forces Velocette decided that they could live with the torque reaction created at the rear bevel box. The other factors were first the forces that arose when the throttle was blipped and which caused a BMW to lean to the right when this is done. In practice this is only noticeable when changing down briskly at a low road speed so seldom arose in racing. Finally there were the gyroscopic effects that occurred when the machine, and its fast turning flywheels, was banked quickly into a turn.

Velocette cut both these factors out by adopting twin in-line crankshafts which were geared together to contra rotate. Once this basic idea was adopted the pieces fell into place beautifully. One crankshaft drove back via a clutch into the gearbox and out to the rear wheel. The other could drive a blower for racing or dynamo for the road. The whole engine and gearbox unit was neat, tidy and oil tight while the overall appearance was very up to date and could have continued postwar for many years with minimal alteration.

Just two machines were built, one, the racer, was called the Roarer by Harold Willis while the road version became the model O. Both still exist and while they set out on the same basic layout they differ to a considerable degree.

The Roarer engine was based on the MOV dimensions of 68 × 68·25 mm which gave it a capacity of 496 cc. The two crankshafts were contained in a crankcase that was vertically split across the frame so each was supported as in a single. They were geared to rotate so the crankpins moved apart from top dead centre and the coupling gears were positioned behind the crankcase and enclosed by a casting which extended back to house the clutch.

A one piece alloy block with liners went onto the crankcase with a vertical drive shaft to the cams running up through the centre. The cylinder heads looked much as the KTT but had separate rocker boxes and were individual castings. Each camshaft had a bevel gear bolted to it as normal and both meshed with the drive shaft one.

Less usual was the reversed cylinder head with exhaust pipes running straight back from the rear. This suited the layout for the blower with a long inlet pipe to damp out gas pulses running over the engine and any over-heating problem was to have been dealt with by liquid cooling. With the design committed this was changed to air which was to give some difficulty.

The camshaft drive was from a shaft set high in the crankcase on the engine centre line and this was driven by spur gears from the front of the right crankshaft. The left one drove the oil pump and the lubricant was contained in a bulbous casting which bolted to the front of the engine and doubled as an outer timing chest.

At the rear a muff coupling drove the blower from the right crankshaft and the muff was skew gear cut to drive the magneto. The left crank drove the clutch and this in turn an all indirect four-speed gearbox. The output shaft ran above the input so lined up nicely with the left rear fork leg down which it ran to the rear bevel box.

The cycle parts were more conventional with a duplex frame to suit the engine unit and girder front forks. Rear suspension was by rear fork controlled by air springs and oil damping while both wheels had full width hubs.

Power output was 38 bhp when the machine was practiced during the 1939 TT but later development work pushed this figure up to 54 which would have been competitive with the Gilera, at that time the top racing 500. The war and the postwar ban on blowers plus pressing commercial factors prevented the Roarer ever running in a race.

The model O started from the same point with

in-line, contra rotating crankshafts but from then on differed, even to the point of the direction of rotation of the shafts. The crankcase was a barrel form with a rear wall and the engine was all plain bearings. The coupling gears went at the front and the camshaft was driven by duplex chain. It lay on the centre line high in the case with a distributor driven from its tail.

The block was in iron and the head alloy and both were one piece castings. Overhead valves were fitted operated by the four pushrods which sat in a bunch in the middle of the engine and reached the valves by long rockers. Twin carburettors went behind the head and two low level systems dealt with the exhaust gases.

A dynamo was driven from the left crankshaft and the clutch and four-speed gearbox from the right. The final drive was by open shaft with couplings to a bevel box designed to accommodate solo or sidecar gear pairs.

The frame was also unusual for it was a duplex cradle to suit the engine unit and supported this on rubber mountings. At the rear the subframe was not tubular but stressed skin pressings, as had been tried earlier, with slots for the top suspension mountings. These allowed for load variations and had springs with friction dampers. At the front went girder forks and although saddle and pillion pad were separate they were fitted as a two level dualseat.

The model O was intended to be a 500 but the prototype was built to 74 × 68·25 mm dimensions which made the capacity 587 cc. The power was sufficient to push it along at over 90 mph which indicated 30 bhp and the engine was silky smooth in use.

For all that it was a complex machine and would not have been cheap to build. In the early postwar world it was more important to produce numbers for anything with two wheels and an engine would sell and there was little call for Velocette sophistication. Thus the firm concentrated on its singles while it geared itself up for a new step into the world of the flat twin.

2 | The LE—The policeman's friend

The flat twin LE Velocette was announced in the motorcycle press on 28 October 1948 and went on show at Earls Court from 18 November that year. This was the first exhibition to be held for ten years so excitement ran high on that score alone but one of the undoubted stars was the Velocette.

The LE was the result of ideas and ideals that went back some 20 years and of management commitment without precedence in the motorcyle world. Velocette were not a large firm so their resources were limited but the Goodman family used them to the hilt in their attempt to make the machine for everyone.

The aims had been suggested and mulled over for a long time and were a carrot that lured many a company into trouble as it sought to build a product acceptable to the mass market. Many were either too cheap and crude to be reliable, too costly or simply too much like a motorcycle. The attributes needed were in the main self evident with easy starting, easy parking, low noise level, simple controls, reliability, economy, weather protection and easy cleaning all appearing on the list. Included with the original set was electric lighting and by the 1940s this need could be considered to become reliable electric systems. Finally good handling was called for although the mass market would never know the difference.

In late years this list was modified with no

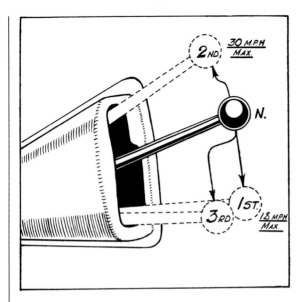

The car type gate gearchange used on the early LE

through the whole firm and to their agents and dealers. The latter were nearly all enthusiasts running typically smallish businesses seeped in oil and perhaps not best suited to retailing a mass market machine but they tried hard.

Hard commerce meant that Velocette had to recoup their tooling costs quickly so the original price was high. In those days reputable businesses paid their bills whereas 30 years later an accountant could well have guided them otherwise. In 1948 you paid your way and that was how the Goodmans lived. They banked on enough sales early on which would then have allowed a reduction on the price tag but this was not to be.

vibration, long life, reasonable power and shaft drive being added to the virtues. It was also expected to be a reasonable price.

There was only one way to achieve this last and that was by production on a large scale with the machine designed for this and the components made by modern tools. Assembly would have to be on a line which was a system not used at Velocette until after the Second World War.

The idea of producing such a machine fascinated Eugene Goodman and so he set Charles Udall at work to translate the dream into reality. The first decision was to use a flat twin engine and this was adopted to minimize vibration. The side valves came to keep the width down and water cooling to reduce noise. From that base many of the machine's features followed automatically.

What made the LE so special went beyond the fresh concept to add in the basic Goodman philosophy of doing the job correctly and honestly as they always had. It was an outlook that ran

Control layout taken from the owner's handbook for the 149 cc model

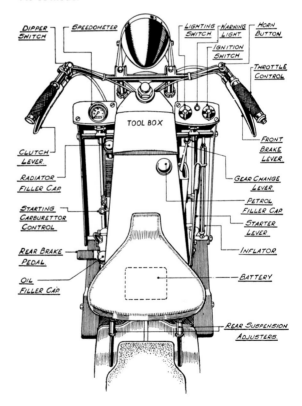

Like many a mass market Mr Everyman machine before it the LE failed. Not totally as it sold well for such a radical design and well by normal motorcycle standards. Unfortunately this was not enough by a long chalk as success depended on the machine reaching out into new markets and it was really too much of a motorcyle do do this.

It also reflected too expensively the Goodman determination to do it right and much of the money they spent in achieving this was wasted on the mass market. The styling was rather odd which put some off and too much of the mechanics could still be seen in an era when much of the mass market took a pride in not being able to understand machinery. It was many years on before technical jargon, albeit often misquoted and misunderstood, became part of the marketing ploy.

The traditional agent's shop with its dirty floor and rows of motorcycles was no attraction either to the mass market man or woman fresh from the car salesroom or the electricity board shop. They were to wait a year or two and then take to the scooter. These may not have steered, braked or handled like an LE while they were noisy, vibrated a bit at speed and needed servicing but they had style. They could also carry a spare wheel, just like the car, were marketed to attract and the lost attributes were never missed as they had never been known.

At the other end of the market older riders tried the LE and while many liked the concept they would have liked some more power as well. Not because they craved high speed but many felt that a better margin on acceleration could be safer on occasion and it is always nice to have a reserve of power—just in case.

The traditional Velocette owner just kept right on running his now very traditional overhead valve single with its odd clutch and his fellow riders in the local club kept their BSA, Triumph or whatever. None would be seen on the LE for then anything under a 350 was considered a lightweight and not for serious motorcycling. Only masochists toured Wales on a 197 cc two-stroke and took three weeks to do it.

At the bottom of the market there was a mass of prospective customers who needed transport to get to work. They could not afford a car and for many the bus, train or tram was not easy to use. Many managed with public transport and others with a bicycle but for most the LE was too expensive.

Those that did turn to powered two wheels bought a BSA Bantam or one of the many Villiers powered lightweights. Even where the LE was financially possible it was still viewed as a motorcycle and everyone knew you got cold and wet on them. There was no screen for face and hands so the use of large mudguards and built-in leg-shields did little to alleviate the weather problem. From this came a need for heavy clothing, with more expense, and the difficulties of keeping clean for the office worker. This was an era when a collar, tie and sobre jacket were the norm and even a garment as loud as a blazer would bring a frown to the office manager's face.

The thought of staff appearing in full motor-cycling gear was enough to label those who did as odd and thus not fitting for promotion. It took the scooter to break away from this and finally the scooterette in the form of the Honda Cub to produce a true mass market machine that was to sell in millions all over the world for over a quarter of a century.

Velocette were not to succeed but they did not fail for the LE was a true landmark in the history of motorcycling and possibly no machine was made with such idealism and honesty behind it. At the time of its debut it received a great deal of publicity in fields quite outside its own specialized one so with its show launch it got off to a good start but somehow the public were never convinced that it was the answer to a transport problem.

In later years it received a fillip when the police took them up for local patrol work to sup-

**Cut-away line drawing of the complete machine in its
original form**

F.W. BEAK

Above **On test with** The Motor Cycle **late in 1948 with the results published one week after the model announcement**

Right **The slots which allowed the rear suspension to be altered to suit its load**

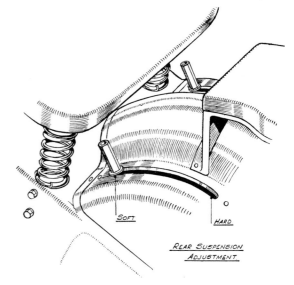

REAR SUSPENSION ADJUSTMENT

plement and sometimes replace the man on the beat. For such work the LE excelled with its whisper quiet engine and easy handling. It allowed a constable to move about his patch quickly without disturbance at night and the machines became known as Noddy bikes. While the name may not have been first choice for the rider it was excellent for Velocette for nothing sticks in the public's mind like a nickname. The police business kept the company going for a good while but finally the law came in from the cold and a new name was coined—the Panda car. With it came finis for the LE.

The LE Velocette was designed as an entity so that engine, gearbox, drive shaft and bevel box were effectively one unit which combined with the structure of the cycle parts. It was thus a far cry from the separate engine and gearbox installed in a, usually rigid frame built up from tubes brazed into forged lugs.

A competition success in 1949! V. Lee with his 149 cc LE in the Bukit Batok hillclimb, Singapore, where he took the 'up to 250 cc' class in 85·5 sec. for the 880 yards. Ftd was 44.2 sec

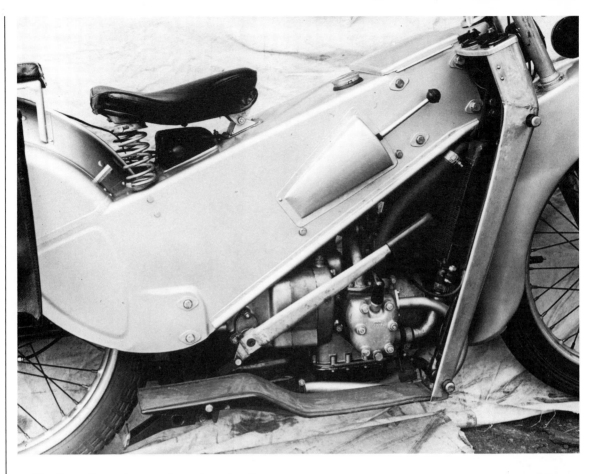

The flat twin-engine was based on the dimensions of 44 × 49 mm to give a capacity of 149 cc. The in-line crankshaft was of built up construction and to keep the cylinder offset to a minimum a roller bearing big end was used. The two crankpins were formed in one with the centre disc and set at 180 degrees to one another. A bobweight was a push fit onto each pin after assembly of the big end and was slotted through so that after alignment it could be clamped in place by a pinch bolt and locknut. The junction of pin and bobweight was then drilled twice and two hardened dowels pressed in to lock the parts.

As the centre part of the crankshaft had to be drilled during assembly and to aid its manu-

Right side of the early LE showing the gear lever and the link between hand starter and centre stand

facture the big end rollers did not run directly on the crankpins. Instead a hardened and ground sleeve was pressed onto them and the 28 uncaged rollers in each bearing ran on that. They ran direct in the steel connecting rods and these had bronze small end bushes.

Each piston was a Y alloy die casting with split skirt and unusual in that a one piece core was used in the die that formed it. In part this arose from its small size and also due to this the gudgeon pins were fitted with bronze end pads and not retained by circlips. It was considered that clips would reduce the bearing area hence the full length, fully floating pins. One scaper and two compression rings were fitted to each flat top piston.

The pistons ran in cast-iron cylinders with integral water jackets. Each cylinder was held to the crankcase by five studs and was deeply spigoted into it. The upper face, when installed, carried the inlet port and one water hose connection while the front face carried the exhaust and a second water connection. Both these cooling connections were tubes pressed into the casting to leave a protruding diameter for the hoses to couple to.

The cylinder heads were cast in light alloy and were held down on a copper-asbestos gasket by six studs. They incorporated water passages and

Early LE with lid and saddle raised. One battery terminal is very close to the body and note 'Players Please' in glove box

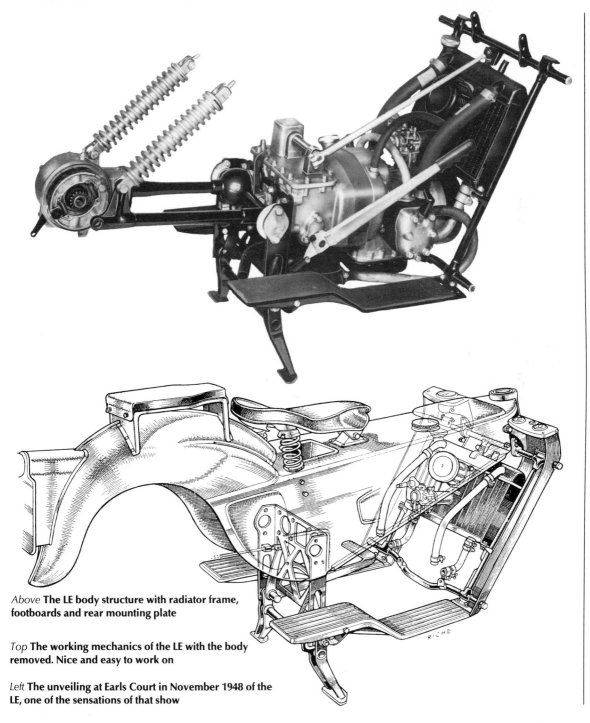

Above **The LE body structure with radiator frame, footboards and rear mounting plate**

Top **The working mechanics of the LE with the body removed. Nice and easy to work on**

Left **The unveiling at Earls Court in November 1948 of the LE, one of the sensations of that show**

31

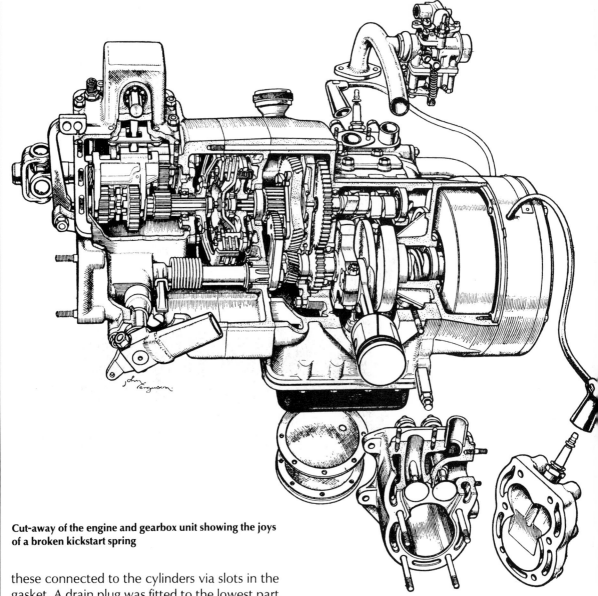

Cut-away of the engine and gearbox unit showing the joys of a broken kickstart spring

these connected to the cylinders via slots in the gasket. A drain plug was fitted to the lowest part of the head and a 10 mm sparking plug fitted at an angle near the vertical. Plug types listed were the KLG type TEN L30, Lodge CL10 and Champion Y7.

The compression ratio was 6:1 and the combustion chamber formed over the valves with

the plug between them. Part of the head spigoted into the cylinder with the gas guided by the chamber shape into position. The valves were inclined to the bore which helped to achieve a

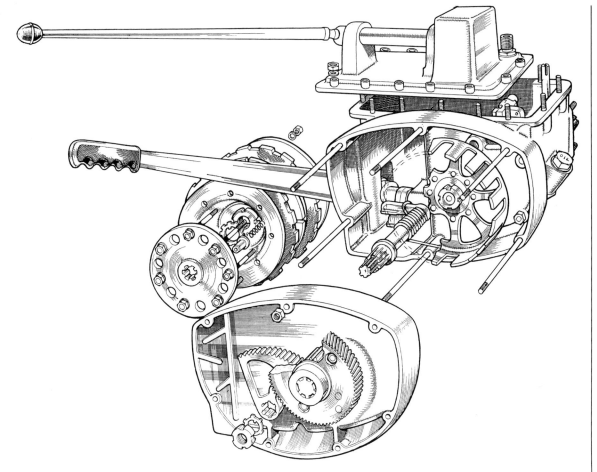

The clutch and transmission castings, also the starting mechanism

compact combustion chamber, enabled more water to be flowed around the valve seats and conveniently pointed them at the camshaft set above the crankshaft on the engine centre line.

The valve seats were machined in the cylinder casting and the guides were in cast iron and pressed into place. Both valves were the same and restrained by single springs retained by a collar and split cotters. Between valve stem and camshaft went square section tappets with radiused ends working in cast iron guides pressed into the crankcase while valve clearance was set with an adjuster screw in each tappet locked by a nut. Access was via one of two plates each held to

the top of the crankcase by four studs. The camshaft itself was a forging with all four cams formed in it and ran in a pair of ball races in the crankcase. It was driven by a pair of spur gears positioned at the rear of the engine within a timing chamber.

The crankcase was cast in light alloy and of barrel form open at the front. The rear wall carried ball races for crankshaft and camshaft

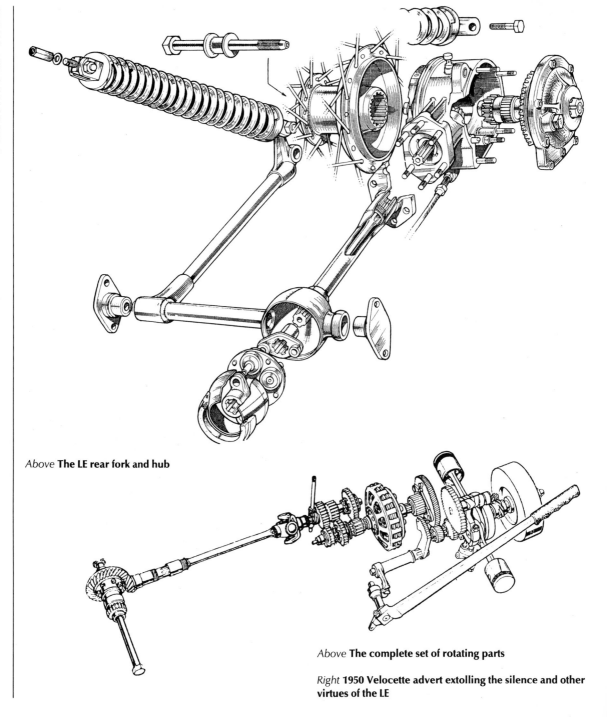

Above **The LE rear fork and hub**

Above **The complete set of rotating parts**

Right **1950 Velocette advert extolling the silence and other virtues of the LE**

TECHNICAL EXCELLENCE EXEMPLIFIED

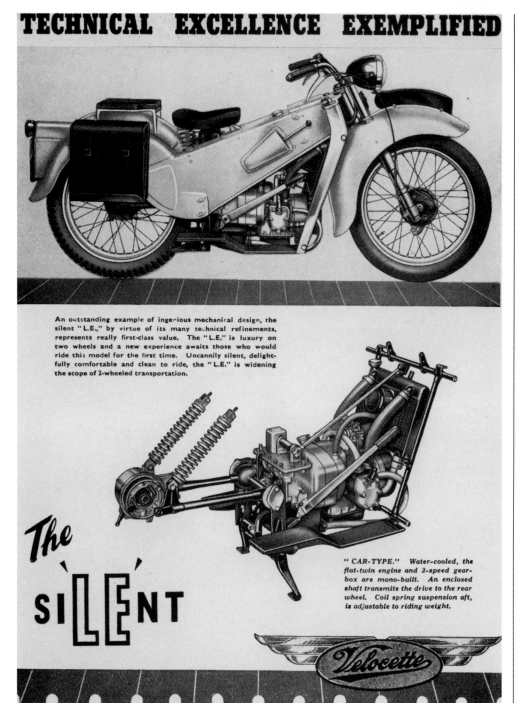

An outstanding example of ingenious mechanical design, the silent "L.E.," by virtue of its many technical refinements, represents really first-class value. The "L.E." is luxury on two wheels and a new experience awaits those who would ride this model for the first time. Uncannily silent, delightfully comfortable and clean to ride, the "L.E." is widening the scope of 2-wheeled transportation.

The SILENT

"CAR-TYPE." Water-cooled, the flat-twin engine and 3-speed gearbox are mono-built. An enclosed shaft transmits the drive to the rear wheel. Coil spring suspension aft, is adjustable to riding weight.

Velocette

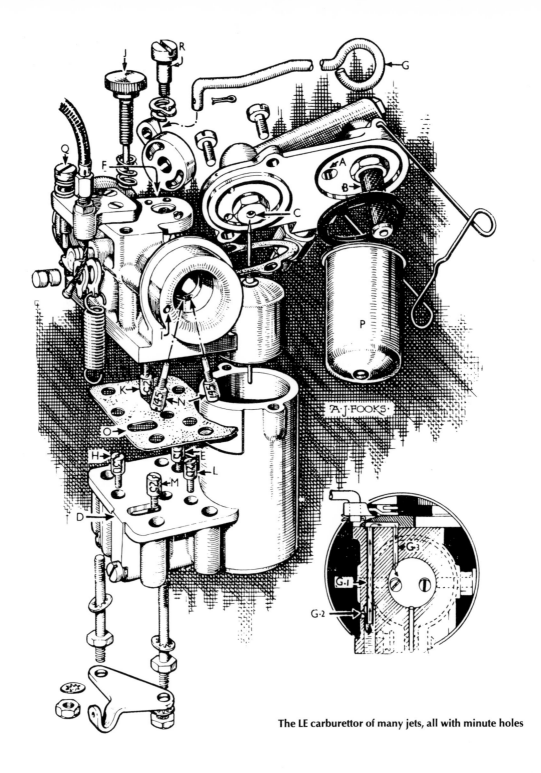

A·J·FOOKS

The LE carburettor of many jets, all with minute holes

and a rim at the front took the forward camshaft race. This rim was scalloped at two places to allow the connecting rod small ends to pass through when assembling the crankshaft into place. The sides of the crankcase were machined for the cylinders and the base for the sump. At the rear of the casting an oil filler orifice with screwed cap was positioned on the left and the casting continued a little to the rear to provide the timing chest and primary gear case.

A separate plate bolted to the rear of the crankcase to house a tail support bush for the crankshaft and a forward one for the clutch shaft. Aft of it went the primary gears. At the forward end of the crankcase went a further casting to close it off and to carry the two front ball race main bearings and an oil seal.

Between the two mains the crankshaft carried a worm gear which drove the oil pump which was fixed to the main bearing support casting. The pump was a single gear pair type which ran submerged in the oil of the wet sump system. Ahead of the crankshaft oil seal went a flywheel and its chamber was sealed off by a BTH generator unit whose rotor was keyed to the crankshaft. Around this were positioned the high tension coil, distributor, contact breaker, ignition condenser and dynamo cut-out. All very compact with a cover on the front to give access for servicing.

A single lobe cam was carried on the crankshaft nose and was at first driven via an automatic advance mechanism. This was later dispensed with and early service manuals contained instructions on how to lock the mechanism solid. The cam opened a single pair of points and a gear fixed to it meshed with a distributor above it which sent the current to each plug in turn. Included in the generator housing was a points gap gauge which was a piece of steel shim of the correct thickness sprung between two cast ribs on one side.

The lubricating oil was carried in a pressed steel sump held to the underside of the crank-

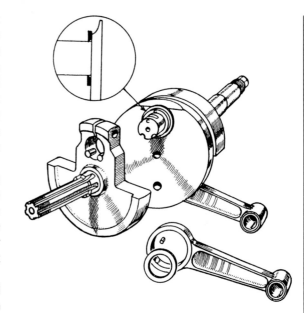

The clamped and dowelled crankshaft assembly

case against a cork gasket by 16 studs. The sump had a drain plug in one corner and a plate which held a circular filter in place around the oil pump inlet. The oil was fed under pressure to a jet set directly beneath the crankshaft centre web and this was scalloped away adjacent to each big end. Thus the oil was directed to the bearing surfaces which while rather crude was better than the petroil two-stroke engines lived on and saved drilling all those long holes in tough crankshaft steels.

In addition to the jet mounted in the pump body oil was also taken via a pipe to the rear support plate where it fed the plain main bearing and jets to the camshaft gears and primary drive. The remainder of the engine was lubricated by splash and mist and all oil drained back to the sump. Engine breathing was by a chimney formed in the back of the crankcase on the right and sealed off by the primary drive case. Within

Offside of the 1951 model

G.Beresford

LE 192

the chimney were cast three angled faces for the oil to condense onto and then drain back and at the top a union and pipe took any overflow discreetly away.

The cooling system was pure thermo-syphon without pump or thermostat. The radiator was made with right and left finned tube assemblies joined by one piece head and bottom tanks. Its cap was sealed with a gasket and a release valve was fitted in the top tank. One pair of pipes connected each cylinder to the radiator and that completed the system.

The carburettor was anything but simple and was specially designed by Charles Udall and once developed was made by Amal. The problem was its small size which ruled out the normal motorcycle units and only left stationary engine ones. These gave anything but the smooth running and slow, dead reliable, tick over demanded by Velocette so something fresh had to be evolved. The result had a horizontal choke with butterfly throttle, integral float chamber, lever controlled cold start system and a built-in filter chamber nearly as big as the float one. The reason for this was the minute jet sizes used which were very sensitive to dirt and a fair amount of work was needed to develop it. The jets were all fixed and numbered four while three spray tubes were fitted.

The carburettor sat above the engine attached to an induction pipe which spanned the two cylinders. This gave a rather long intake length but could not be avoided without fitting twin carburettors which would have raised other problems. On the intake side the carburettor was connected by hose to the centre of the radiator which was an enclosed space. Above the intake hose an air filter was fitted and by this means the induction side was preheated from the radiator.

The exhaust was simple with one exhaust pipe on each side which curled under the cylinder and ran back to a common silencer. This was lined with glass wool with a single outlet curled

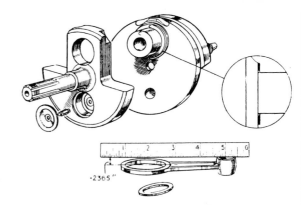

Above **Revised crank web with sludge trap and Velocette style pressed assembly**

Left **A 1952 LE at the Paris Show and fitted with twin extra lights. Lovely shine on the legshields**

round to the right and was very efficient for the low noise level of the LE was one of its outstanding features.

One that was to give Velocette problems for the helical primary drive gears at the back of the engine were noisy at first and not easy to quieten to the low ambient level of the machine. On anything else their whine would have been lost in the general clatter but if all is quiet then anything can intrude. A clock in a Rolls Royce and, for a while, the contact points in the LE. So the gears had to be attended to.

They gave a reduction of about 3:1 so neatly reduced the clutch speed to an acceptable level and moved the drive line out a little and up to the rear wheel centre. The clutch was positively normal by Velocette standards with two friction plates and eight compression springs to clamp it all together. It lived in a dry chamber behind the primary gear one and took the power in from the one side and sent it out to the other. It was lifted by a lever at the back of the gearbox which moved a pushrod.

The clutch housing was part of the gearbox casting so in all there were four alloy pieces joined by studs and bolts to form one compact assembly to take the mechanics and the external

1954 LE200 with oil filter mounted on cylinder head and chrome plated body edging

items. The gearbox was a three-speed, all-indirect type and effectively a cross-over drive as the input came in at the front and went out at the back. It also went out on another shaft laid alongside and further out from the input to line up with the rear wheel drive.

To connect the two shafts were three pairs of gears to give the ratios with top gear less than unity to compensate for the primary and final reductions. Both gear shafts ran in ball races and the gears were selected by a car type mechanism. Velocette decided that the customer for whom the LE was designed would not appreciate his or her shoes being marked by a foot pedal so they plumped for hand change. In addition they decided that the same customer would want to be able to slip into neutral from any gear just as with a car and not be forced to go through the box and then hunt an elusive neutral.

So hand change it was with a long lever on the right working in a gate to move one of two

selector forks. Gear positions were as on a car with first to the left and down, second to the right and up with third straight down from second. Unlike a car a ball joint was not used at the base of the lever to allow it to rock from one selector

The water heated induction manifold and moulded hose adopted for 1955

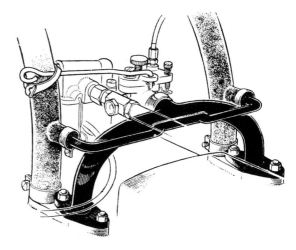

Above **Sectioned LE shown at Earls Court in the early fifties**

Below **The cast light alloy rear fork adopted during 1955**

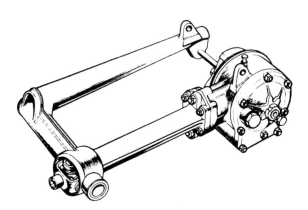

to the other. To minimize the lateral movement the lever was rigidly fixed to one end of a cross shaft with the selector finger at the other. The assembly was mounted in a tube containing a low friction bearing which allowed the shaft to turn and to slide easily from side to side. This side movement enabled the finger to pick up the correct selector fork assembly and move it. Each fork assembly had a spring loaded plunger set in it to locate into one of three grooves in the rod they both moved on. This acted as an index plunger to hold the gears in mesh but no interlock was fitted as is normal in a car to prevent one selector moving of its own accord.

The low friction bearing comprised a tube with flared ends pierced to locate six ball bearings at each. This sat on the shaft and in the tube to give the required effect very simply. The whole

Left **The Noddy bike around 1955—better than walking the beat**

Right **And on the move under training**

mechanism was assembled to the gearbox top cover and this held down by 14 studs. The top cover also carried a bushing for the speedometer drive shaft which was positioned vertically in the left rear corner of the gearbox and driven by a skew gear splined to the output shaft. The speedometer cable thus rose from the rear of the unit to run in a smooth curve to the instrument head.

As well as a hand gearchange the LE also had a handstart as the Goodmans felt that kickstarting did not enhance the owner's image. A lever of some length went on the right of the machine and was pulled up to start the engine. The first stage in connecting this pull to the crankshaft was by a pair of arms in the clutch chamber. These sat at right angles to one another with the first keyed to the handle shaft so it pointed forward. The second sat above it and pivoted with its shaft which sat in-line with the machine so the arm pointed out to the right.

It was this second arm shaft that carried the starter return spring and its forward end passed through the casting wall into the primary gear chamber. There it carried a quadrant gear splined to it and this meshed with a gear running free just behind the driven primary gear. This had twin spring loaded pawl levers pinned to it to take the starter pull and via the gears turn the engine over. To assist the engagement of the quadrant gear its first tooth was spring loaded and able to float.

The mechanism thus gave primary starting which was a useful feature to offer riders of perhaps limited experience as stalling in traffic was then much less of an embarrassment. It had one further trick up its sleeve as the handle was linked to the centre stand to retract this if it had been left down in error. To make parking easy and to aid the retraction the stand was in effect a pair of props made in one piece so the machine could roll onto it with ease.

A universal joint went just behind the gearbox with its working centre positioned on the rear fork pivot. The coupling itself was a disc with four rubber bushes bonded into it with opposite pairs facing fore and aft. These pins mated with flanges splined in one case to the gearbox output shaft and in the other to the drive shaft. This ran down the left rear fork leg to the bevel box which bolted to the leg.

The box was a light alloy casting and housed spiral bevel gears that gave a reduction of 3:1. It differed in detail from the prototype built late in the war but in essentials was the same. Both pinion and crown wheel shaft were carried in twin races and the housing had lugs cast to it for the rear brake cable and the left rear suspension unit. The crown wheel shaft was machined as a gear at its inner end to pick up with the rear wheel hub. The rear brake was mounted on the inner face of the casting with the cam lever working within a recess cast in the base of the housing.

The engine, clutch and gearbox were built in one unit and the shaft drive and bevel box required to sit in a precise relation to it. This was done by bolting a good sized steel pressing to the back of the gearbox and giving this two rear pointing flanges. Holes in these served to carry the pivot points of the rear fork and thus the whole engine and transmission became a single package.

The frame that carried it was unique in its day and gave the machine its very distinctive line. The main part was a 22 swg steel pressing to which was welded the very deep and wide rear mudguard. The result was a beam of inverted U section and at the front was bolted a welded steering head assembly. This comprised a tubular headstock with braced flanges which ran back to mate with the main frame body.

Just behind the headstock a twin compartment toolbox was set into the top surface of the frame and welded in place. It was closed by a lid hinged on the right and held down by a clip. Behind it within the frame pressing went the $1\frac{1}{4}$ gallon petrol tank which comprised two half pressings welded together and supported by

Bernal Osborne of *Motor Cycling* **testing an LE early in 1955**

welded-on straps which bolted to the main pressing. The filler neck protruded through a rubber grommet set in the frame and was closed by a half turn cap. A single pipe connected the tank to the petrol tap which was screwed into the carburettor.

Behind the tank the saddle front pivot was bolted to the top of the main pressing with attachments for the two saddle springs further back. Between them and thus beneath the saddle went a battery container welded to the pressing with its contents restrained by a simple strap held by two bolts. Two further pressings were

welded to the rear mudguard, one on top to act as a carrier or to mount a pillion pad, and the other at the rear to carry the rear number plate and lamp.

The pressing took the loads of the rear suspension units, but not at fixed points. Instead, Velocette used the system already tried on the model O and had each unit inclined forward to locate at its upper end in a slot cut in the mudguard. Thus by moving the unit fixing from one end of the slot to the other the suspension could be varied from hard to soft or anything in between. They did remember in the handbook to remind owners that both units had to be set to the same point.

The remaining parts of the frame comprised a tubular assembly at the front, two footboards with mounting brackets and the rear engine pressing already mentioned. Although not obvious at first glance the whole engine and gearbox unit was resiliently mounted with rubber bushes and washers at each fixing. Thus at the rear the pressing in which the rear fork pivoted was held to the back of the gearbox by seven studs with these bushes. The connection to the main frame pressing was by the two bolts on each side which held the pivot pins in place as they went through the body as well.

At the front the tubular assembly was bolted to the main frame. It comprised a top cross tube, two down tubes and a lower cross one to form a square and in this went the radiator supported on two side brackets and one top one, all with rubber buffers incorporated. The lower cross tube supported the front of the engine, again with rubber insulation between the two, and was located fore and aft by the footboards. These were bolted to the tubes and also to the rear engine pressing to form a rigid structure. The boards had two levels to accommodate both rider and passenger and the working surface was covered by a ribbed rubber mat.

The tubular assembly also supported a pair of light alloy legshields of angular form but as they were joined to the footboards they did offer good weather protection. Each had a small top panel fitted to it and that on the left carried the speed-ometer while the right one had the ignition and lighting switches plus a warning light. A tyre pump was clipped inside the right legshield.

To augment the comfort of the rear suspen-sion a Velocette saddle was fitted. This com-prised an alloy seat pan with sponge rubber cushion with detachable waterproof cover and was supported by a front hinge and two coil springs. Behind this the passenger was offered a rather thin pad which bolted in place and would

Osborne had to contend with a good deal of ice and snow during the 1955 test but had no great problems thanks to the LE's handling

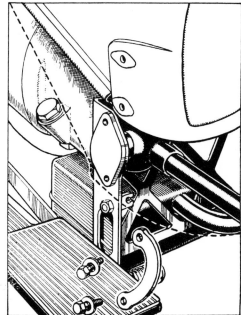

Above and right **Tubular frame serrated joint and rear fork fixings**

Top **A 1957 model with steel panniers and very stepped dualseat**

not have enticed many to ride far. The pad was more of a luggage carrier and in this role supplemented the panniers fitted as standard. To support the bags a mounting tray was bolted to each side of the rear mudguard while the bags

themselves were quickly detachable.

The centre stand was pivoted in the rear frame pressing below the rear fork pivot and the rear fork built up from tubes and lugs. It pivoted on bronze bushes and the front end of the left leg

Above **1958 MkIII with four speed gearbox and kickstarter**

Right **How the changes were fitted in and linked to their pedals**

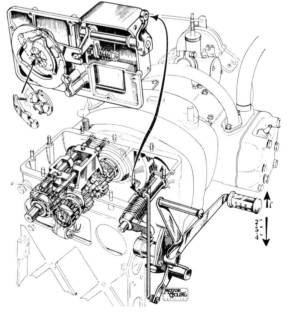

was expanded to surround the universal joint. A further shroud and seal connected it to the gearbox casting. The rear units which controlled the fork movement were made by Velocette and contained springs only without any damping other than friction.

The front forks were boringly normal by LE standards, just telescopics with the oil in them, more for lubrication than damping. What was different for a small capacity machine was the use of taper roller bearings in the headstock, another indication of the firm's determination to do the job properly. Otherwise fork construction was conventional with bronze bushes supporting the sliders and the springs held by scrolls top and bottom. Again not quite the norm for a lightweight and neither was the use of a leading axle

with the front wheel spindle ahead of the fork tubes.

A really massive front mudguard was fitted to the underside of the bottom crown and was thus a sprung part. In order to cover the wheel it was deeply valanced and its width was such to enclose the fork legs as well. It carried a number plate with licence holder built into its tail and no mudguard stays were used. At the rear of the machine a simple plate was provided for the registration number.

Both wheels had offset hubs spoked into light alloy rims carrying 3·00 × 19 in. tyres. In line with Velocette racing experience the front was ribbed and the rear studded, another indication of their wish to produce a machine with good handling. The hubs contained single leading shoe brakes which worked in drums of 5 in. diameter with a width of ¾ in. The wheels did not interchange but both were easy enough to remove. The rear brake pedal went on the left above the footboard

1960 LE showing the switchgear in the headlamp shell

where it did intrude a little on the available foot room.

The handlebars were well swept back and bolted to the forks in one fixed position. Both clutch and front brake levers worked on welded-on pivots and the twistgrip was the axial type so the bars were very clean. To the controls on them had to be added a dipswitch on the left and a horn button on the right. The horn itself went between the fork legs just above the front mudguard.

The 6 in. headlamp was mounted on lugs welded to the handlebars on production models but the prototype had two lamps with one mounted on the top of each legshield. They were rather small and no doubt Velocette found as did others that a fixed light is not a blessing on a motorcycle.

The electrical system had one merit not usually provided on machines with a dynamo and coil ignition. This was an emergency start position for the ignition switch in those carefree days was simply a switch with a knob to turn. No ignition key or lock then. If the battery was flat the machine could be push started and also, if needed, it could be run without the battery. In the latter case the lights would not work so this use was restricted to daylight hours. No stop lamp was fitted.

So the machine for everyone was born and its type letters came from the prosaic name of Little Engine (Light Engine from one source) and were simply a convenient way of distinguishing its parts and tools from other and larger engine items. The idea stuck so the detail parts all carry LE numbers with assemblies prefixed LAS. Service tools are sensibly prefixed LET which makes them easy to select from those used by the K or M models.

The list price of the LE was £99 10s all inclusive at a time when nearly all other firms quoted the mandatory speedometer as an extra and would not have included panniers as standard fittings. Sadly for UK buyers most machines were initially destined for export and even if available there was purchase tax to add on which pushed the price up to £126 7s. 4d. At that time a typical lightweight fitted with a Villiers 197 cc 6E engine was sold for just under the £100 barrier and in 1948 the extra £26 or so was a very real consideration. A much tougher blow was the appearance of the BSA Bantam in the middle of 1948 as although originally for export only, by the end of the year its UK list price was established at £76 including tax but not the speedometer.

The public liked the new Velocette. The LE was a hit on its debut at Earls Court and came across as a dignified personal form of transport. The finish helped with the main body and front mud-guard in silver grey, alloy legshields and wheel rims and minimal chrome so the machine looked sombre and respectable, an important point in those austere years.

The problem for Velocette was making them for they were a complete departure from the firm's traditional singles and they only had a year or two's experience of running a production line. Prior to this each machine was assembled on a trestle. Early plans were to drop all the singles and concentrate on the LE to the tune of 300 machines a week but this proved unrealistic. Up to then production rates had been around 100 a week and to treble this figure with a totally new model was not on.

BSA might have done it but they had more space, more money and more production line experience so the simple Bantams poured off their lines in 1949. At Velocette it was another matter altogether. The singles continued in production to keep the money rolling in and the initial LE line proved to be unworkable so output was low. The line had to be re-planned and as it got underway the inevitable teething troubles also had to be dealt with. In time these matters were solved and production settled down but never at 300 a week. The best figure was 169, all LE models, and the best when singles were built at the same time was 158.

A week after the announcement of the model came road tests in the two English magazines. *The Motor Cycle* was lent registration number HON 611 from which they reached a maximum of 48 mph while *Motor Cycling* received HON 612 and ran it through the timing lights at 52 mph. However, over a flying quarter mile they too recorded 48 mph. Both magazines achieved consumption figures over 100 mpg and excellent braking distances when stopping from 30 mph.

The outstanding feature of the LE was its silence. In an era of rorty singles and poping two strokes it glided along as if the engine was not running. While in city traffic it was often inaudible to the rider or anyone else for that matter

Above **The MkIII in two tone finish**

Right **An LE engine unit with complete transmission on a typical test rig with wires and pipes in all directions**

and more than one pedestrian walked in front of one because it was not heard. The firm used this attribute in their advertising with the 'siLEnt' feature given prominence.

The LE was also very smooth and completely free from vibration thanks to its engine layout. This rather accentuated a quick clutch and some transmission judder when moving off, often caused by the light clutch action and the difficulty of judging engine speed without the 'benefits' of noise and vibration.

Much appreciated by the motorcycle testers was the handling and suspension which was fully up to Velocette race bred standards. A feature that the aimed for customer would not realize existed at first until such time as the basic stability and ease of cornering had impressed itself firmly.

The riding position seemed to work well for most as feet could be moved to the most comfortable position on the boards. The gear-

change worked well. The legshields did their job and kept the rider's feet dry even when the road was soaking wet. The headlight had a good beam. The variable rear suspension unit setting worked well in practice to cope with the carriage of passenger or when used in the 'soft' solo position.

Really the LE Velocette was an extraordinary achievement by the Goodman family. It would have been something special if built by BSA, Triumph or AMC, all of whom had real resources, but from a small company it was a true act of faith. What is also so special is that the Goodman's so very nearly got it right for in its two decades plus in production the model was basically unchanged. Economics rather than technical design were the forces to beat it over the years.

Not that the first models were without problems and some adverse comments. It took some very careful gear manufacture to get the primary

pair to run to an acceptably quiet level. And before long the limited acceleration and hill-climbing performance began to pall. The 50 mph maximum was fine—it was just that it took too long to reach and gradient and wind had too much effect.

There were no changes when the 1950 programme was announced but the price had risen to £148 6s 9d while for 1951 it went up another tenner. However, for that sum the buyer got another 43 cc as Velocette had responded to the requests for more power by boring the cylinders out to 50 mm and a 192 cc capacity.

They also brought in a good few other internal changes although on the outside all looked as before. The crankshaft was stiffer with the main-shafts forged integral with the bobweights and the crankpins pressed into a taper interference fit. The big end diameter increased as did the small end which had an improved bush and the gudgeon pin was retained by circlips.

The tappets were changed to a round section with flat feet and the cam profile adjusted to retain the timing but give a more rapid opening. The same cylinder head casting was used but machined to increase the combustion volume so the compression ratio remained as before. Lubrication was improved by an increase in oil pump capacity obtained with wider gears and the crankshaft oil feed revised.

The original oil jet was replaced by blanking plug and all the oil now went to the reduction gear plate. This retained the bleed to the timing gears plus a pipe to take oil up to fall into the clutch housing bearing. The main oilway was via the plain crankshaft bearing into the rear main-shaft with a restrictor jet at the front end of the shaft in the bobweight. The oil was thus directed in a steam into a cup set in the centre crank disc and from this oil holes fed straight into the big

A pair of LEs in the factory on the assembly line

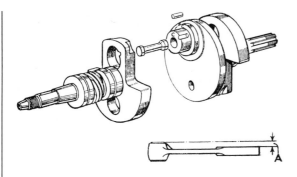

The plain bearing crankshaft. The plug in the crankpin is used to form an annular oilway

in place of the BTH although the latter continued in use for some time. The Miller did away with the distributor, cut-out and brush gear as the current came from an alternator with external half wave rectifier mounted beneath the petrol tank and behind the carburettor.

An automatic advance mechanism and points cam went on the front end of the crankshaft and opened a single pair of points which fired two high tension coils mounted on the stator plate. This simple system with an idle spark was to

ends. Just aft of the restrictor jet the bobweight was drilled through the weight and sealed by two washers held in place by a common central rivet.

From engine number 12640 some machines were fitted with a Miller type AC3 generator unit

Right **The zener diode heat sink plate under the toolbox. The attachment of the headstock can also be seen**

Below **LE cooling and exhaust systems**

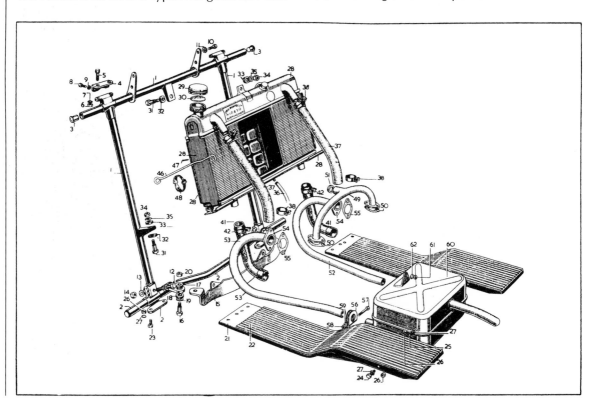

become common practice two decades later but was unusual in 1951 when it was feared that it would upset the intake and exhaust process occurring in the cylinder.

The stator plate thus acted as a useful mounting for the coil ignition items but on its other side it carried the coils for the alternator. Within a few months it was found that if the battery was connected the wrong way round it demagnetized the flywheel so a protective circuit breaker was added and the unit became the type AC3P. It was fitted from engine 15840 for 1952 but was itself superseded by the AC4 late in 1953. From this point only Miller systems were used although the BTH was not officially removed until 1956. The AC4 added a ballast resistor in the supply line to the ignition coils and the alternator was wired to a full wave rectifier mounted within the frame above the gearbox on the right side.

From the first appearance of the Miller generators the switch panel was revised. The right switch became one with six positions which were: park, emergency ignition, off, ignition and charge, head and rear, pilot and rear. A centre key allowed it to be locked in either the park, when rear and pilot lamps came on, or off. In those days it was a legal requirement to show lights when parked on a road at night, hence the arrangement. To the left of the switch went an ammeter while the warning lamp was deleted. The left panel remained as it was.

On the transmission side the rubber universal joint became a Hooke type with needle roller bearings and the clutch was fitted with heavier springs. The second gear ratio was raised and detail changes made to the gearbox and rear bevel box. The machine was listed as the LE200 and its numbers carried a 200 prefix.

The change gave it the boost it needed as while *The Motor Cycle* did record a maximum

The 1965 rear brake pedal with toe guard. Note spring connection to stop light switch

of 57 mph with the larger engine the more important aspects were the improvements in acceleration, on hills and when carrying a passenger. Fuel consumption increased but only to about 95 mpg when the performance was well used. With minimal care over 100 mpg would be obtained.

In all other ways it was as the original 150 model and even the substitution of ball bearings for taper rollers in the headraces went unnoticed. This occurred in the first place due to supply difficulties so for some years either form of bearing was used but in the end the lower cost of the balls made their use inevitable.

While there was only the minor modification to the Miller generator for 1952 there were a good number of changes in 1953. The main one in the engine was to plain bearings for both the mains and the big ends and to keep these in good condition a pressure oil system with external filter was adopted. This last went onto the engine from number 19609 but the bearings were not listed prior to 19917 so came in about halfway through the year.

The oil filter was a cylindrical container which bolted to the front three right side cylinder head studs. It contained a fabric element and was connected to the system by pipes running to base and top. In the oil circuit it went between the pump and the gear plate from which the oil went exactly as before. Some 300 engines were built in this manner.

The plain bearing crankshaft was built up much as before with the centre disc formed in one with the two crankpins and the bobweights integral with the mainshafts. Bearing sleeves were pressed on for both mains and big ends and oil holes drilled through to feed all working surfaces.

The oil pump remained where it was but was joined by a maze of pipes in the sump. The first took the oil from the pump to the pressure release valve which was bolted to the outside of the crankcase beneath the right cylinder. An

Left side of the LE in 1965 fitted with dualseat and panniers

adjustable valve let excess pressure back into the sump while the remainder was taken to the filter and then returned to another crankcase connection. This ran it to a distributor block and from this three more pipes connected to the bearings and the reduction gear plate.

Other changes were simpler with a third clutch plate being added and a hole about 2 in. diameter appearing in the left side of the main frame pressing. This gave access to the speedometer cable and was filled with a blind grommet when not in use. The link between the stand and the starting handle was deleted as the feature was not found to be needed and was a nuisance when servicing the engine. The rear brake shoes were widened to 1 in.

Finally, late in the year, the tubular frame round the radiator was modified. Major servicing of the LE was done by removing the entire body structure from the engine transmission assembly. To ease this task the lower cross tube of the frame was made a separate part from the two down tubes and mated to them with split lugs. Each of these had deep serrations to engage with its other half and a single bolt held them in place so they carried the loads.

The changes for 1954 were simple with the front brake shoes joining the rears at 1 in. wide while access to the speedometer cable and the resited full wave rectifier was improved with a modified battery box. With this change the hole in the left side was deleted.

Early in 1955 there were further engine changes and at number 22637 the camshaft was modified to plain bearings. At the same time an oil feed was taken to the rear one and the camshaft made hollow to supply its front bearing.

Some 40 engines later the big end bearings were widened by $\frac{1}{16}$ in. and these went in from engine number 22678. This rather typified the Velocette practice of incorporating improvements as they came along rather than waiting for an annual changeover. It does mean that an owner has to be a little careful as to specification, engine and frame numbers and spare parts. A situation not helped by the numbers not being the same on all the early 200s and the ease with which they could be switched. Also the frame number went on a plate riveted to the toolbox lid and was thus easily lost.

Also for 1955 there were changes to the cooling system with moulded rubber pipes replacing the steel pipes and connecting hoses between the radiator outlet and the cylinders. Above the engine the hoses running up to the top of the radiator had small outlets added at the rear. These connected to a cross pipe which was welded to the back of the induction pipe to act as a heater to prevent icing in the system.

A two-level seat was listed as an option and had a pronounced step between rider and passenger. Like the saddle it replaced it pivoted at the front and was hinged up to give access to the battery. The saddle remained the standard fitting but the rear frame was modified to accommodate a revised rear number plate and its support became a separate part bolted to the main frame pressing. The pillion platform also became a bolted-on part.

To brighten the model up two-tone colour schemes were offered with the choice of secondary finishes in ruby, green or blue. This was applied to both mudguards and the lower edge of the main frame with a black separating line. The finish was embellished with chrome-plated strips fixed to the lower edge of the frame and further plates running from the rear fork pivot area along the lower edge of the rear mudguard

Close up of points on front end of crankshaft

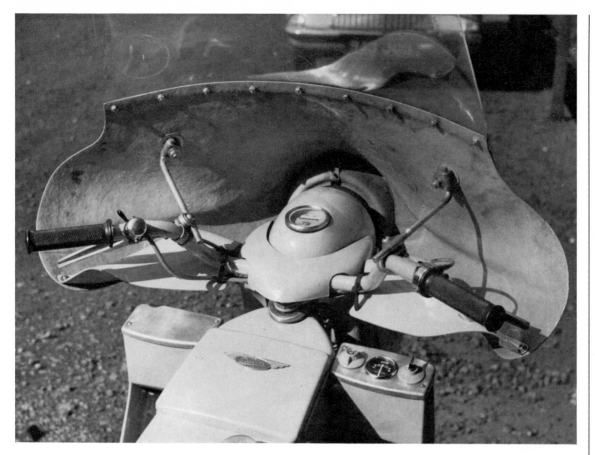

Left **Modified body and the big 12 volt battery. Photo also shows seat construction and cover**

Above **The Lucas switches used with the 12 volt system**

to the pannier frames. The wheel rims were by now chrome plated so steel rather than the original light alloy.

In the middle of 1955 at frame number 22046 a major change was made to the rear fork when a light alloy gravity die cast part replaced the original fabrication. Although the appearance and function were as before the two parts did not interchange.

For 1956 taper face, chrome-plated top piston rings were fitted and the tank capacity increased although there was still no reserve provided.

Externally a new design of streamlined pannier boxes became available as an extra and these had a rounded form to blend with the machine. In pressed steel they looked rather out of place on the angular LE and for the old-fashioned purchaser the old style panniers remained available. A further two-tone finish in dove grey with the standard silver grey was added to the lists and the legshields were no longer polished but painted to match the mudguards.

In the middle of the year a luggage carrier available in a colour to match the machine was added to the list of extras but had gone again when the next year's models were described although it was to return. Before then, in July 1956, various changes were introduced which were to continue on the 1957 models.

The most noticeable were to the wheels which gained full width hubs using the same size of brakes and fatter tyres of smaller diameter. These became 3·25 × 18 in. and their introduction was preceded a little by a change to an Amal Monobloc carburettor in place of the fixed jet type which had been in use since 1948. The new unit had its own air filter and silencer so the separate one attached to the radiator was dispensed with and the radiator amended accordingly.

With the new carburettor came a repositioned fuel tap and this had an extension bar attached to its operating lever with access to this via a hole cut in the left side of the main frame pressing. Similar to the hole provided for a speedometer cable access in 1953 but further forward to suit the installation.

The final change introduced at that time was less obvious and affected the oil pump and the sump. The pump was altered to incorporate a circular intake filter as part of the assembly and this removed the need for the gauze set in the base of the sump plus its attendant mounting, cover and fixing nuts. Without this the sump became a simple pan and gained slightly in oil capacity.

The 1957 changes were less spectacular and all concerned the optional features. New was an oil gauge which came with necessary pipe, unions and a new legshield panel to mount it next to the speedometer. For tourers there was a spare petrol can, or as Velocette put it, a special auxiliary fuel container, which came with a bracket which clipped to the standard pannier frame. For disabled riders, for whom the LE had many useful features, there was a kit to fit the brake pedal on the right side of the machine. Finally, yet another two-tone paint option was

listed in polychromatic olive green.

Motor Cycling road tested the machine early in 1957 and found that the changes to tyre size and carburettor type had no real effect on its performance at all but the petrol tap was easier to operate than before. When cold, and under frosty conditions, it took several pulls on the starting handle to draw the mixture in and fire it up. Speed, consumption, brakes and handling remained as they were.

When the 1958 range was described the LE had no changes listed and only a reduction in the two-tone options. These became silver grey with green, polychromatic green or blue as alternatives to the standard silver grey.

However, in November 1956 the company had introduced a sporting flat twin called the Valiant which is described in detail in the next chapter. This followed the LE concept in many ways but had an air-cooled ohv engine, four-speed gearbox, footchange, kickstarter and conventional cycle parts. While the engine, other than heads and barrels, looked much like the LE it had a greater offset between the cylinders which had many repercussions on detail parts. For all that there were many common items.

With the Valiant running nicely Velocette were then able to take the next logical step and fit it with LE barrels to produce a revised model. They had found that any attraction the hand starter and gearchange had tended to be offset by a wish to keep both hands on the bars when changing gear. So there was no obstacle to using the newer features and the opportunity was taken to bring in some other changes to revise the appearance a little.

The engine used the same dimensions as before and was built along the same general lines. The four-speed gearbox bolted to it and the gears were selected by a face cam mounted in the top cover with the positive stop mechanism. An external link connected to the gear pedal while the kickstart spindle went just above this lever. The speedometer cable came out from the front left corner of the gearbox casting and as it swept up required the petrol tank to move right a little to give it room. The petrol tap and its attendant access hole in the main frame pressing also went to the right side.

A minor change was the removal of the induction pipe heater which had been found not to be needed with the Monobloc carburettor. This instrument was set round to be square to the pipe to avoid mixture bias while the pipe was angled across to match the cylinder offset. The silencer top was indented to give clearance for the deeper gearbox casting and the pressing that bolted to the back of the casting was revised and held by four bolts only rather than the seven used up to then.

There were also changes on the cycle side with the main frame modified to remove the gear lever aperture. A shroud was fitted to the upper front forks and this cowled in the handlebars and their fixing and was extended to meet the headlamp shell which it also supported. The shell carried the speedometer in its centre which thus became much easier to read and the ignition and light switch ahead of it on the right with the ammeter matching it on the left. The handlebars were of a new shape and less swept back than before.

The top panels of the legshields were no longer pierced as standard but the oil gauge and a left panel to hold it remained available. The legshields themselves were altered so the right one carried the horn and the left one the licence holder. In turn this meant a new front number plate without the rounded end that it had carried from the first model.

The new machine was typed the MkIII and made available in the standard silver grey or the two-tone colour options of the older version. This became known as the MkII and continued in production for those who still wished to have three speeds, hand change and hand starting. Or maybe just to clear stocks as it went from the lists in September 1958 after selling another 100 or so machines that year. A few three-speed MkIII machines were also built in later years to individual order.

Once again January saw *Motor Cycling* testing the LE, this time in MkIII form. Naturally in many respects the behaviour was unchanged but the provision of four gears did allow much brisker riding on occasion. Second was good for 40 mph so fine for traffic work where the legendary LE silence made the use of full throttle no problem. Third gear took the machine to 50 mph and was close enough to top to work well in hills and against high winds. Otherwise it was the mixture as before but improved with time.

In the spring of 1958 the LE was modified in the clutch area to adopt the Valiant bonded clutch plates and to harden the working edges of the driven plates and the bell slots they moved in. Also the oil system pressure release valve had a plunger substituted for the ball bearing but the spring pressure on it remained adjustable.

During the year *The Motor Cycle* also reported on the MkIII LE and confirmed just about all the points their rival publications had made. The machine had now reached its tenth birthday and was fairly set in its format for its remaining years. For 1959 a windscreen appeared as a much needed option and early in the year the piston rings were modified to increase their radial thickness.

That aside, the model continued for 1960 but for 1961 the headlamp rim was modified, a stop light was listed as an option and the metal panniers were dropped. There were no more alterations for some little while and by this time the motorcycle market was changing and shrinking. Velocette were able to keep the LE in production by selling them in considerable numbers to police forces.

Over 50 forces in Great Britain had taken up the LE by 1959 and the sight of the police constable running round his beat quickly and quietly had become common. At first they continued to wear their normal tall helmet but later this was

Earls Court late in 1966 with the Met showing both Triumph Saint and LE Velocette

adapted into a crash helmet. In either case the nickname of 'Noddy men' was inevitable and hence the LE became the Noddy bike which passed into common usage and was a boost for motorcycling in general.

The police and public liked the machine for it enabled the man on the beat to cover it quickly and to move to incidents under radio guidance from his station. The public were pleased to see a man on the beat once more and to be able to talk to him if needed thanks to the very quiet running engine.

Thus by 1964 most LEs were built for the police but a few were still sold to the general public and both had their last major changes introduced for 1965. Many of these concerned the

electrics which became a 12-volt system using Lucas parts throughout, a switch to that maker having been made during 1964. A zener diode went under the toolbox to control the current and twin batteries were fitted. As options the buyer also had the choice of two larger capacity batteries or a single and even larger 12-volt one which was standard for the police model. With the 12 volts came a new switch system which went on the right legshield top panel. This carried the ignition switch on the right with removable key and off, on and emergency positions. On the left went a light switch with off, side and headlamp while between them went an ammeter. This left the speedometer alone in the headlamp shell.

Within the engine the timing gears were made wider and the oil feed into the crankshaft increased while the barrel castings were revised to modify the coolant passages so the gasket area around them was increased. Behind the gearbox the propeller shaft was waisted to increase transmission flexibility and in the rear bevel box went a more robust crown wheel and pinion with longer teeth of thicker tooth form. The carburettor became an Amal type 19 with slightly larger bore.

Externally the main frame pressing was made of a heavier gauge but whether this was to cope with weighty police constables or simply to compensate for wear on the press tools was not indicated. A detail change was to a heavier rear brake pedal which had a toe guard to keep the well-polished size ten police boot from scratching itself on the cylinder head nuts.

After that there were no changes for 1966 but 1967 brought some added stiffening to the underside of the body. From then on the LE continued as it was, still offered in its two-tone finish but in much smaller numbers. Most of the 1969/70 production was to fulfil a large order for the London Police and in February 1971 the end came for the factory and with it the end of the whispering watercooled flat twin.

The company had been in some financial difficulties during the previous year or so and by the end of 1970 liabilities were on the point of overtaking assets. So the family, true to their honest ways, went into voluntary liquidation and paid off all creditors their full 20 shillings in the pound. They thus missed the introduction of decimal coinage to the United Kingdom so worked in good old-fashioned pounds, shillings and pence to the last. The final seven machines were assembled at the direction of the liquidator to meet long standing orders and most went to well known Velocette dealers in the London area.

Not long after the factory closed. It was pulled down to allow redevelopment of the site and so disappeared the Hall Green works of the Velocette company.

3 | Valiant—neat and nice

The Valiant was announced in the press in November 1956 so was first seen by the public at the Earls Court Show held later that month. It represented Velocette's attempt to meet the demand for sports machines of under 250 cc and to provide a livelier performance from their flat twin design. With that as a basis the result was a sophisticated and therefore expensive motorcycle and coming from Hall Green there was no attempt made to cut corners and save money by cheapening the design.

Velocette were able to build the machine in this manner because they already had the LE factory tooling which could be used or adapted to suit. This enabled the Valiant costs to be kept within reason and gave a bonus in reducing those of the LE as more machines came off the same tooling. Unfortunately the benefits of doing this brought the limitation of keeping to the LE capacity which put the model in line with the Triumph Tiger Cub and numerous Villiers 197 cc powered lightweights.

Naturally the Valiant found itself at a price disadvantage and those buyers who appreciated the extra refinement and could or would pay for it were none too plentiful. All too many dealers found that customers would admire the Valiant at £185 but put their money down for a Cub at £144 or go for a full 250 cc model such as a Francis-Barnett Cruiser at £174.

If Velocette had been able to stretch the capa-

The Valiant loop frame that was one factor in the good handling

city to 250 cc this would have put them in contention with a different range of models and at a level where more customers would have been prepared to pay a premium for the highly respected name. It would also have given the machine a power boost which could have put it at the forefront of the top end of the 250 cc market.

This in turn could have had further repercussions for in 1961 came, in the UK, the restriction of learner riders to 250 cc and with it a demand for sporting 250s. It was a market area that was cost conscious but craved performance and while the Velocette would always have been pricier than some they must have benefited from that legislation. As it was, the learner market dismis-

sed the Valiant as too small, too costly and not quick enough.

Within the trade many felt that the company's mistake was that once it was realized that the Valiant could not stretch beyond 200 cc then it should have switched to a 250 single and built the MOV model once more. That could have used much of the single cylinder tooling and was a known and liked machine but it was not to be.

So Velocette decided on the Valiant and Charles Udall, their technical director, was given his brief. Use the existing engine jigs and fixtures and what you can from the LE. He in turn decided that over 200 cc the gyroscopic effects of the flat twin layout would become noticeable which seems a spurious idea in view of the smoothness of the then current BMW twins. The suspicion is left that this point was voiced to mask the capacity limitation of the tooling as ultra smoothness was not really that essential for what was a sporting engine.

Much more logical was the adoption of overhead valves which widened the power unit but not to an unacceptable level and the use of air cooling. The quietening effect of a water jacket was not necessary and in fact could have been a sales deterrent while air cooling was cheaper.

The layout of the Valiant engine and transmission was just as that of the LE but many of the details differed in some way or another.

SECTION THROUGH PORTS

ECCENTRIC PIN
ADJUSTMENT

The Valiant engine with four speed gearbox

Beginning at the crankshaft this had to be stiffened to cope with the added power and at the same time the big end bearings were widened. The result was a greater offset between the cylinders and this required the crankcase to be lengthened.

The crankshaft was built up from a circular centre web, two crankpins and two bobweights with integral mainshafts. The parts were simply pressed together using the Velocette technique

of a taper fit on pin and in bore of 0·008 in. per inch of length. This meant that initially the pin would drop into place and touch at a predetermined axial point. Given that this was of the correct length then pressing the pin home gave the right interference fit. As had been used by

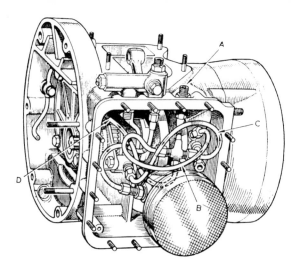

The snakes nest of oil pipes revealed when the sump came off

the firm for a quarter of a century.

The big ends were split shells pressed into the eyes of the steel rods and the small ends were bushed. The mainshafts had hardened sleeves pressed into place to provide the main bearing journals with the details as for the LE. The gudgeon pins were retained by circlips and the pistons had split skirts, shallow dome crowns with valve cutaways and two compression rings and one scraper each. Initially only the top ring was taper faced but in production both were and the top one chrome plated from the start.

The cylinders were cast in iron as there was no call for light alloy on the score of heat dissipation with the flat twin layout and the weight saving would have been minimal but expensive. The pushrod tunnels were formed by pressed in tubes, light alloy at first but steel in production, as this made it easier to provide the desired air flow around the barrel. Five studs held each to the crankcase while four studs went into each cylinder head to attach it to the barrel. Thus all the fixing nuts lay between the cylinder fins.

The cylinder heads were cast in light alloy and unlike the barrels were handed left and right. The valve seats were shrunk into place and further steel tubes enclosed the pushrods to the rocker box floor. The inlet ports were offset so the mixture flowed down into the combustion space but the plug remained on the upper side where it was better protected and more accessible, Technically incorrect but proven by tests to have no significant effect.

The valve gear was conventional with the camshaft driven as on the LE and running in plain bearings. The cam form gave more lift and an extended timing as would be expected. Flat base tappets were used, free to turn in iron guides pressed into the crankcase, and had screwed in pins in their top faces. These engaged with the hardened steel endcaps of the light alloy pushrods.

At the top end were compact rockers which pivoted on an eccentric pin fixed in cast in pillars in the head. Rotation of the pin enabled the valve gaps to be set. The valves worked in pressed in guides located by circlips and each was restrained by two springs retained by collar and split collets after initial models with only one. The springs were a light interference fit to each other which helped to damp out any tendency to surge. The whole of the rocker box was enclosed by a simple domed cover held in place by two screws.

The front of the engine carried the same Miller AC4 generator as the LE but fitted with a different advance unit to suit the needs of ohv. The crankcase was essentially the same although longer but did have the tappet access holes blanked off by inserts in the casting dies. By changing these the holes could re-appear for use with the MkIII LE.

The lubrication system was as for the LE plus a feed to the rockers. The pump with its filter, the release valve, the oil filter and the distribution block all did the same jobs. The one variation was to move the filter to a position under the

clutch housing as the cylinder head location was no longer suitable.

The rocker feed came from the top of the timing chest and an external pipe ran to each side from a double banjo. Each pipe curled down under the inlet port and up again to the cylinder head where an internal drillway connected it to the upper inlet rocker pin post. The oil ran down the pin into the rocker bearing and a pressed in pipe connected the inlet post to the exhaust one. After use the oil drained back to the sump via external pipes from the bottom of the cylinder heads.

Behind the crankcase went the step down helical gears and starter quadrant and behind them the clutch. This had three driven plates with Feredo friction rings bonded to them but was otherwise as the LE. The starter was essentially as in the LE but with a kickstart lever in place of the hand one and this fitted to a square ended shaft rather than being secured by a cottar pin. Its movement was rather short and restricted by a lug forged into the pedal which came up against a rubber buffer stop after a meagre arc. It did, however, turn the engine

The Valiant in 1957 with its engine bonnet carrying horn and licence disc

through one cycle just as the hand lever had.

The clutch drove a four-speed gearbox which was sufficiently compact to fit in the same space as the three speeder. The casting was similar but revised to only have four fixings on the rear face and for the speedometer drive to emerge at the left front corner. The drive was taken from the nose of the output shaft and mounted in the separate front bearing plate. This item was otherwise as before and carried both front ball races for the gearbox shafts, the rear ones fitting into the shell.

The compact gearbox design came from using a single row of dogs in the middle of the input shaft to drive either the third or fourth speed gear either side of it. A selector formed as a duplex bridge located the two free running gears either side of this feature and moved either one or other to lock to the shaft. The matching gears on the output shaft were formed as one so only needed a single selector fork to move them on their splines on the shaft. At either end went free running gears which the centre double one engaged dogs with to provide the first and second ratios. The free gears were themselves driven by fixed ones splined to the input shaft.

The two selectors slid on rods set in the top of the gearbox and were controlled by a face cam pivoted in the gearbox top. Above the cam went the positive stop mechanism which was moved by a horizontal shaft set across the cover with an external lever on its right end. A link connected this to the gear pedal which was pivoted on the frame.

From the gearbox the power was transmitted down the left leg of the cast light alloy rear fork via a universal joint and propeller shaft. At the rear went the bevel box as on the LE complete

with brake and drive to the quickly detachable rear wheel. The fork pivot was as for the LE together with the seal to protect the universal joint.

The complete engine and transmission unit was mounted in a duplex frame with single top tube. This supported the unit with the mounting under the front of the crankcase and from the back of the gearbox to the rear fork pivots. The frame was well gusseted around the headstock area and the subframe was formed in one with it. Footrests, pillion rest brackets, centre stand, rear brake pedal, gear pedal and a neat chrome plated tubular crash bar all bolted into place.

Front suspension was by LE forks painted to match the rest of the machine. They carried a sports mudguard with a cross stay on each side

A speed run during a 1957 test when the Valiant managed 67 mph. Reversed bars and racing leathers could add another 10 mph

Valiant and early Vee Line in 1957

Early Valiant advert plugging its points

and the front number plate. At the rear a pair of Woodhead-Munroe spring units with hydraulic damping controlled the movement of the pivoted fork.

Both wheels were as for the LE and thus had full width hubs laced into WM2 steel rims fitted with 3·25 × 18 in. tyres. Both brakes were of 5 in. diameter with single leading shoe operation and 1 in. width. The rear wheel was protected by a simple blade mudguard supported at the tail by a stay on each side that also acted as a lifting handle. The mudguard carried a boxed in rear number plate with rear lamp as standard or stop and tail as an option.

The petrol was carried in a three-gallon tank rubber mounted on two blocks on the top tube and with two buffers in the gussets. These braced the tank tunnel to prevent it turning on the tube. The tank was held in place by a quick release centre strap that pulled down on a rubber pad which sat between the two central seams. The strap was formed to locate on pivots set either side of the headstock and its tail had a slot which went onto a hook at the rear of the tank. The strap was chrome plated while the tank was decorated with round plastic badges and kneegrips. There were two petrol taps and the tyre pump was carried between lugs on the underside of the tank.

One of the main styling features of the Valiant was a two piece cowling or bonnet which

The Vee Line model with its substantial fairing and tall screen

enclosed much of the crankcase and gearbox. On the prototype it also covered the single carburettor which was connected to the two inlet ports by a rather lengthy induction pipe. To suit the ohv layout it had to be longer than that used by the LE and was linked to the exhaust to gain some mixture preheat. In all, this added up to rather a lot of complication which gave a throttle response that was scarcely quick enough for a sports machine.

Thus Velocette chose the simple way out and fitted twin carburettors, each on its short inlet stub and served by one petrol tap. The exhaust side was equally simple with each cylinder head

fitted with its own exhaust pipe which ran back under the barrel to a torpedo shaped silencer.

The cowling was therefore revised to suit the twin carburettors which sat outside it. On its left front side the licence disc holder was mounted and at the front went the electric horn so that for once this item looked built in and not hung on as an after-thought.

A toolbox was fitted on the right side of the subframe with a lid held by a single screw. In it went the battery while for those with more to carry a matching box to fit on the left was offered as an option.

The handlebars simply bolted in one position to the top of the forks and had welded on pivot blocks for brake and clutch levers. A combined horn button and dipswitch went on the left and

the main lighting and ignition switch in the head-lamp shell on the right. It was balanced by an ammeter on the left and behind them was the speedometer. The rider was provided with a dualseat but the pillion footrests were an extra.

The electrical system was as on the LE with coil ignition, full wave rectifier and six-position switch to control it all. The stop lamp switch went just behind the rear brake pedal on the left, the pedal being connected by cable to the wheel.

Within a short time of its appearance the rear mudguard was altered to fit it with valances and the lift or support stays altered to act as grab or lifting handles. In this context the Valiant was unusual in that the foot peg on the centre stand was on the right side. This was to allow the machine to lean to the left when a wheel was being removed or replaced.

The crash bar already mentioned was an optional but worthwhile fitting and in addition to the left toolbox, pillion rests and stop light, the Valiant owner could also have a pair of chrome-plated tank panels. These enhanced the standard paint finish which was either in dark green or black with the tank lined in gold.

Road tests followed but not until late August 1957 when the two magazines published theirs on the same day. On performance they were very similar with 68 mph top speed and 90 mpg consumption although both were rather coy on the second figure and gave their usual fixed speed figures.

The Motor Cycle contented itself with cal-culated maxima in the gears based on the makers' recommended 7000 rpm limit *Motor Cycling* had no such qualms or less of a mechani-cal conscience for they ran their example to 8000 rpm in second and only a 100 less in third which gave them speed figures of 45 and 60 mph.

Both magazines agreed on the excellent brakes and handling but differed on riding position and comfort.

The Valiant made its rider lean forward and as the controls were totally fixed anyone not to the standard size could find too much weight on their arms. The seat looked and felt hard at first but proved good over long journeys as such seats often do. With this 'fast rider' position, good steering, ample ground clearance and a quick gearchange the Valiant was an excellent machine for hastening over highway and byway. Another 10 mph would have helped of course.

As production got underway in the early to middle part of 1957 other changes were incor-porated. The compression ratio settled to 8·0:1 in place of the 8·5 talked of at the launch and the rear units were changed to Girlings with three position load adjustment. To combat some criti-cism of the exhaust noise better silencers were fitted. For the 1958 models a plastic balance pipe was fitted between the inlet stubs and ran across the top of the crankcase. This improved the tick-over and was made available to owners as a modification.

In the spring of 1958 there were further changes as on the LE with hardened driving sur-faces within the clutch and a modified oil pres-sure release valve with a plunger in place of the ball bearing. The engine number location also altered.

The option list extended to add panniers for the Valiant and these went forward with the unchanged machine for 1959. With it came a second model call the Valiant Vee Line which was fitted with a dolphin fairing. This was a fibreglass moulding with bonded in facia panel and glove box. It was of a good size so gave pro-tection to the hands and the legshields went out-side the cylinder heads with apertures for the cooling air to enter.

Vee Line dashboard and cowl over fork top. Does not seem to suit the line somehow

Overleaf **The author on borrowed Valiant at Silverstone where its handling and brakes impressed**

Above **Valiant rear end in 1961**

Below **Right side of 1962 Valiant**

Nice clean Valiant with period mirror added. It hinged in
if needed for small gaps

Final 1963 version of Valiant with small exhaust pipe to
frame brackets

A wide windscreen was fixed to the top of the fairing and behind it the facia was taken back to mask the handlebar fixings. It carried the speedometer, ammeter and switch and below it was the glove box. The headlamp remained in its shell which was mounted on brackets bonded into the fairing so it retained its vertical adjustment although it no longer turned with the forks.

The fairing was attached to the machine at eight points and added 21 lb. to its weight and £21 to the price. For that the owner received the chrome-plated tank panels as standard. From March 1959 it was also available to Valiant owners as an extra.

For 1960 the compression ratio was down a trifle to 7·8:1 and the alternative to the black colour was given as willow green. The Vee Line model was dropped from the list for 1961 and during that year brackets were added to the frame to support the exhaust pipes and two gaskets fitted under each cylinder barrel. To keep the valve gear in the correct geometry a washer was added between the tappet and its screwed in pin and the result of this exercise was to reduce the compression ration to 7·0:1.

A 1962 road test merely served to confirm earlier results with similar performance figures and remarks. The exhaust note was still felt to be 'sporty'. From then on the Valiant continued without change and in the autumn of 1964 went from the list.

Rather a pity for it was a nice machine to ride with excellent handling and many desirable features. Unfortunately while riders asked for shaft drive and a sophisticated specification, few actually got their cheque books out when it was offered. A friend bought one which is how I came to have a ride but he was the only one—so Velocette found, as had others before and after, that it was financially painful to listen to owners and riders.

Still, it was a nice motorcycle.

4 | In Vogue but out of fashion

Perhaps it was the name as well as the price that put customers off the Vogue. Club puns on the name were many and it appeared at a time when the motorcycle and scooter markets were contracting. The machine was a deluxe model based on the LE and aimed at buyers who wanted LE silence with more style but without much dash as there was not a lot 192 cc of side valve engine could do to drag some 300 lb. of machine plus rider along.

Sadly for Velocette there was no such market and their committment to the flat twin cost them rather dearly. The market, such as it was, called for super sports 250s but maybe the firm felt that while an MOV might have been possible, one with rearsets, clip-ons and go-faster tape definitely was not. Certainly not from Hall Green with their tradition of black and gold singles.

The Vogue was first seen at the Earls Court Show late in 1962 when it created a great deal of interest. The appearance was perhaps rather premature as it was the middle of 1963 before production got underway and the first road tests were carried out.

The new model was in essence an LE with fibreglass body which in turn meant a new structure to replace the original main frame pressing. This structure was based on a massive backbone welded to the headstock with a short cross tube just above the rear fork pivot. From this two plates extended down to support the pivot

The twin headlights of the Vogue

Right above **The Vogue which never became the vogue**

Right **Tubular frame and one piece body of the Vogue. Same concept and mechanics as LE, different clothes**

points in the same manner as the other models.

To this basic frame was welded a subframe which at first was a simple loop which ran up and back from the cross tube and then straight back to carry the rear of the bodywork. At the front end of the main backbone were welded brackets to support the radiator tubular surround frame which did the same job as on the LE.

For production the rear part of the frame was modified and made much stiffer. The subframe loop was replaced by two tubes which ran straight back, side by side, to support the body just below the seat pan level. These tubes were welded on each side to short vertical tubes which ran down to the main cross tube and were braced by a pressing set at an angle and which also acted as part of the rear mudguard. The horizontal tubes were contined further forward and braced down to the backbone by a further pressing welded into place.

On top of this frame went the main body moulding, all the fibreglass being designed and made by Mitchenall. This main section ran from head to taillight and was fixed to the frame by

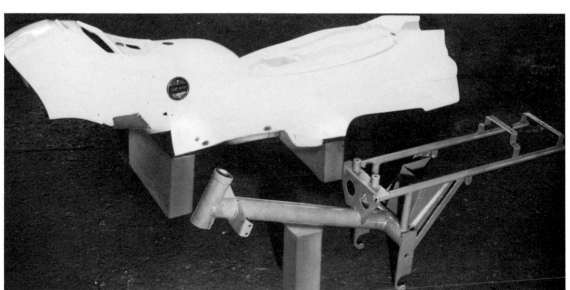

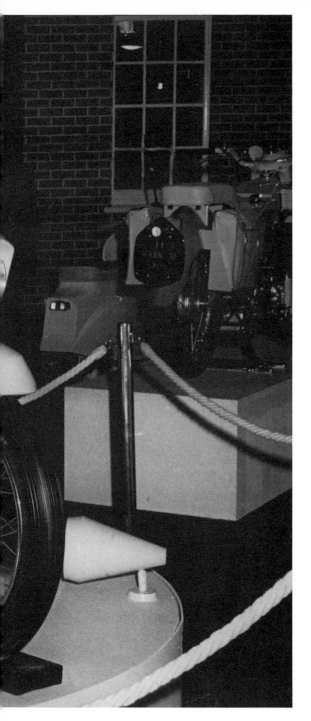

Vogue on show

eleven bolts. All the wiring was carried within it and the 2½-gallon petrol tank was formed in the body during manufacture. At the front end twin headlights were provided for, side by side, and the top surface behind them was formed to carry a windscreen and as an instrument panel. Recesses were moulded into the top of the seat area to accommodate the battery, toolkit, tyre pump and a radiator filler plug.

To the main body were bolted legshields which extended up to the windscreen and down to the footboards. The tops of the legshields were formed into small trays and beneath them on each side was an open glove box. At the front of each box the moulding was formed to carry a direction indicator lamp and these front ones matched at the rear by others set in the main body.

The footboards were much as for the LE but with the rear ends curved instead of being cut off square and with locations provided for the side access panels. These went on each side and were retained by three quarter-turn fasteners. The effect was to fully enclose the mechanics of the machine to produce a design not unlike that of the Ariel Leader.

The dualseat sat on top of the body with a location at the front and held down at the back by a quarter-turn fastener. The filler cap went ahead of it in a conventional motorcycle position with the handlebars on a stem that protruded up through the body. They carried the normal motorcycle brake, clutch and throttle controls with a combined horn button and dipswitch on the left.

The speedometer with distance recorder went in the centre of the instrument cluster ahead of the handlebars and was flanked on the right by an ammeter. To the left went the combined ignition and lighting switch with its detachable lock-

Left **Front end of a road test Vogue in 1964**

Above **Same test showing tools, tyre-pump and battery in moulded recesses and one of the side panels**

ing key as used on the LE. Two small holes were pierced either side of the speedometer and the right one carried the lever to operate the indicators and the left one the warning light for them. The whole instrument panel could be removed as a unit.

Ahead of the panel the moulding was raised up to carry a Velocette badge and in front of that went the windscreen. This extended out onto the legshields so that it protected the rider's

hands. The front of the moulding carried twin headlamps under a styling eyebrow and these were a distinctive feature of the model.

To go with the new styling there was a matching front mudguard possibly even more voluminous than the LE one. It extended well forward and like its predecessor encompassed

Overleaf **Bob Currie road testing the Vogue**

93

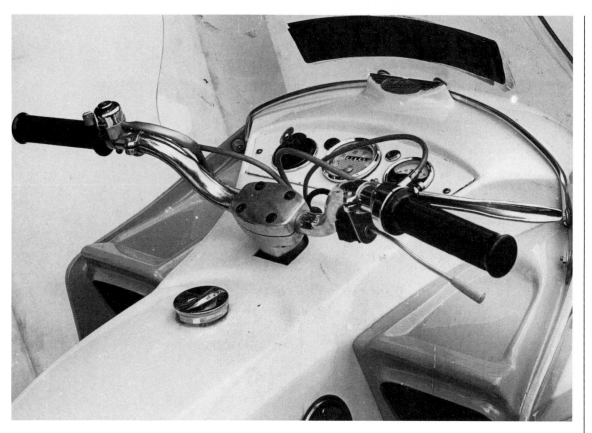

Above **Vogue dashboard and handlebars. Note turn signal control under twistgrip**

Far left above **Right side of Vogue without side panel to show LE mechanics**

Far left **Left side of Vogue; note oil cooler above clutch housing**

Left **Vogue rear showing styling fins, indicators, rear carrier and panniers**

First dashboard with vertical lever indicator switch

Right above **A Vogue with panniers and tank badges in their usual place . . .**

Right **. . . and with them removed. Note dirty sheet background for this photo**

the fork legs. On some machines the front number plates were attached one on each side of the mudguard but others had a single plate fixed to the base of the screen. The rear plate was mounted on a moulded in surface and flanked by stylized tail fins.

Also in fibreglass and an optional fitting were panniers formed to fit to the main body and styled to match it. Each had a locking lid. Other options were a rear carrier and the fitting of a stoplight while both screen and indicators were extras although seldom not fitted.

Under the skin the mechanics were the LE with

a few changes to suit the new application. The whole of the engine, gearbox and rear fork assembly was used and the front forks and wheels were also from the LE. Changes were minimal with the oil filter moved to a position on top of the timing chest and the gear lever

Overleaf **1966 Vogue with short windscreen**

arranged to protrude from a curved slot in the right panel. The position of the rear spring units was fixed which was to give a rather hard ride when solo which improved if a passenger was carried even if this did depress the performance.

The carburettor choke control was on the left and emerged from the main body via a small hole while the petrol tap knob matched it on the right. The latter went between the two top side panel fixings with the panel moulded to clear it so was quite unobtrusive. As with the LE the stand left both wheels on the ground and acted as a dual prop so was very easy to use.

With twin headlamps, turn indicators and a six-volt electric system it was soon found that the standard Miller generator was hard pressed to cope. To deal with this problem many Vogues were fitted with the Miller AC4/PO which pushed out 80 watts and so could. In addition the indicator control became a switch with long lever mounted on the right handlebar so it lay beneath the twistgrip. At the same time the warning light moved over to the right and the small left hole in the panel was blanked off.

Early examples of the Vogue were tested by the press in the middle of 1963 as it went into production and were given good reviews. There were a few minor points that needed attention but the mating of the silence of the LE with style and good handling was applauded. Laced into the comments along with the detail criticisms was the hard rear suspension which was hardly in the touring image and the thought that maybe some more power would help push all that weight and bulk along.

More formal road tests in 1964 showed that 60 mph was about top whack and that main road gradients tended to pull it back to 40. Downhill it would run on a little more but with only 8 bhp acceleration was gradual. Consumption and braking were much as the LE so really

Publicity or road test—110 JOP had to do it all

the Vogue was a town vehicle for whispering about on in silence. It could be used as a tourer but by the mid-1960s one really needed more power to whisk rider and machine along the boring bits to the scenery. Even the pottering in leafy lanes is all very well if you know you can run faster, if you cannot it can lose its charm.

And the Vogue was expensive. The original price a touch under £240 had risen to £246 but with screen, indicators and panniers this rose to £272. At that time the Ariel Leader was £225 and offered far better performance, a Honda CB72 was £260 and a 350 cc Triumph £279. The alternative purchase for a buyer was a scooter and the Lambretta was £200 which left some change for accessories.

Not many Vogues were sold but Velocette persevered with it to try to recoup some of the tooling cost of the moulds. For 1965 it received the engine and transmission changes as on the LE which affected the timing gears, oil feed, coolant passages, propeller shaft, rear bevels and carburettor. It kept its six-volt electrics and Miller generator for another year but in 1966 went over to Lucas, 12-volts and a zener diode.

Sales fell to a trickle and the panniers became a standard fitting but this was of no great help. The machine stayed in the range for a little longer but in 1968 Velocette admitted defeat and withdrew it. Once again it had proved wrong to build to an ideal which the press encouraged but few bought. Fewer than 400 in the total production life and most of them in the first year or two.

So the Vogue withdrew to leave the LE to run on with the singles to the closing days at Hall Green.

5 | Viceroy—the scooter

In November 1960 the traditional Velocette enthusiast, a hard rider clad in his black Barbour suit, received a staggering blow. The LE had been bad enough but time had eased the pain and the appearance of the more normal, if under-sized, Valiant had helped to dull the memory. Then came the final indignity in the shape of the Viceroy, a *scooter* from Hall Green, home of the big single.

Velocette, like many others, had watched the success of the Italian Lambretta and Vespa machines and like most, completely misjudged why they sold so well. Their timing was also out as the two-wheeled market was about to begin a decade long run down and the rather fickle scooter public was about to turn to the Austin and Morris Mini and the Ford Cortina for its transport.

The Viceroy was the Velocette idea of what a scooter should be. They had scant regard for the small wheels, under-damped suspension, doubtful handling, rearward weight distribution and chrome frills and fancies common to most. So they set out to build a machine with scooter style weather protection, a decent size engine to haul the panelling along and, most of all, handling in the Velocette tradition.

The result was inevitably an open frame motorcycle, for the Goodman family and Charles Udall were unable to forget their traditions. They were under some pressure from their dealers to produce something on these lines and at first the request was for an LE turned into a scooter. This was not feasible as the mechanics formed one unit and there was no way of providing the flat platform for the feet which is basic to the scooter. It was tried but the result was a frame too weak for its loads but still without the step through facility. The worst of both worlds.

There was some precedent for the somewhat massive build of the Viceroy as both Zundapp and Maico, both German makers, produced machines of that type. The Maico especially was

recognized as being fast with good handling but was a large machine priced well outside the normal scooter buyers' range. Thus it sold in relatively small numbers to the discerning rider but they were in a minority.

The Viceroy was the last new machine to come from Velocette and took a totally fresh approach to the design problems. For Velocette

Line drawing of Viceroy showing the divorce of engine and transmission

The machine itself, a massive affair

it was unusual in that it had a two-stroke engine and for the first time in their history they used petroil lubrication. By then this was less of a chore than it had been as filling stations were normally equipped to cope with a special pump.

The design of the Viceroy began with the engine position which they insisted had to be well forward to maintain good weight distribution. A flat twin was chosen to keep vibration to a minimum and also because it helped to keep the weight low and forward. Honda were to do the same with their Juno scooter. Capacity was 250 cc to give the required performance and the two-stroke cycle gave simplicity, low cost and kept the width down.

The flat twin two-stroke has both pistons moving together so both fire at the same time to pro-

duce a twin that sounds like a single and has torque like one. The bonus is that one crankcase serves both cylinders so there are no more sealing problems than on a single and the narrow offset gave the smallest of couples as on the other Velocette flat twins.

The Viceroy engine was based on dimensions of 54 × 54 mm so its capacity was 247 cc. The 180 degree crankshaft was built up in exactly the same way as other Hall Green flat twins with a centre circular disc, bobweights with integral mainshafts and crankpins. These had slow taper ends which were a press fit into the wheels as

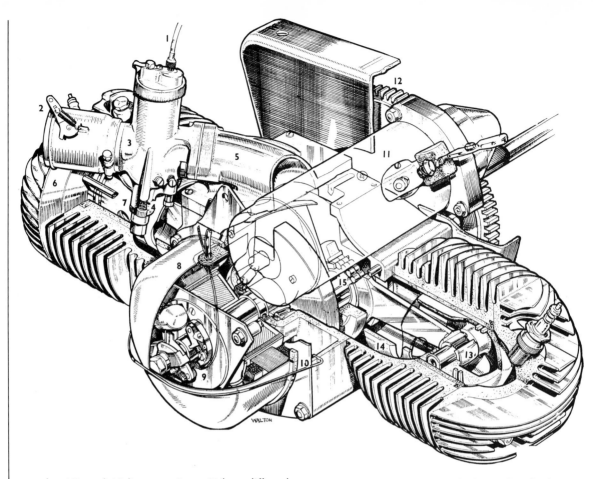

The Viceroy engine with two cylinders and reed valves

on the LE and Valiant engines. What differed were the big end bearings which for the Viceroy were caged, double row rollers. In addition thrust washers were fitted either side of the bearing and these located to the wheels so they did not turn on the pin.

The crankshaft ran in taper roller main bearings which was typical Velocette single practice but unusual for a two-stroke engine. The bearing preload was 0·004 in. achieved with shims behind the outer races fitted into the crankcase.

The connecting rods had needle roller bearing small ends and carried two ring pistons with shallow dome heads. The gudgeon pins were retained by circlips and the piston rings located

by pegs. The air cooled cylinders were in light alloy with iron liners and each capped by an alloy head with part squish band combustion chamber. The compression ratio was 7·5 :1.

The engine breathed through a pair of reed valves mounted on top of the crankcase which kept the carburettor in the centre out of the way and simplified the cylinder casting. Each barrel had its exhaust on the underside and two transfers, one on each side of it. They were inclined to aim the incoming mixture and all port openings were machined in the liner before it was shrunk into its muff.

The two exhaust pipes ran back to a silencer mounted low down on the left of the machine where unfortunately it got in the way of removing the rear wheel. It comprised an alloy end casting which fitted to the two pipes, a cylindrical member containing the baffle assembly and a rear alloy end casting. To remove the rear wheel the scooter owner, maybe in his or her Sunday finery, had first to remove the baffle section and rear casting, neither of which was likely to come away easily or fail to leave its mark on hand or clothing. It was not a feature much mentioned in the salesroom.

The intake side began with an air cleaner

Viceroy transmission and rear swinging arm in one with clutch, gearbox and bevels

attached to an Amal Monobloc carburettor fitted with a cold start butterfly choke. The carburettor was bolted to a light alloy casting which contained a tract which split into two with a reed valve at the end of each. The reeds were stainless steel and restrictors limited their total movement. The complete assembly simply bolted onto the top of the crankcase. This split vertically across the machine so each half carried one main bearing and an oil seal outboard of it.

On the front of the crankshaft and crankcase went a Lucas RM15 alternator and ahead of this went contact points and a cam coupled to an automatic advance mechanism on the shaft nose. A large pressed cover enclosed both alternator and ignition points and was retained by a wire clip. The points fired twin coils wired in series and the generator output was switch controlled and not by a zener diode.

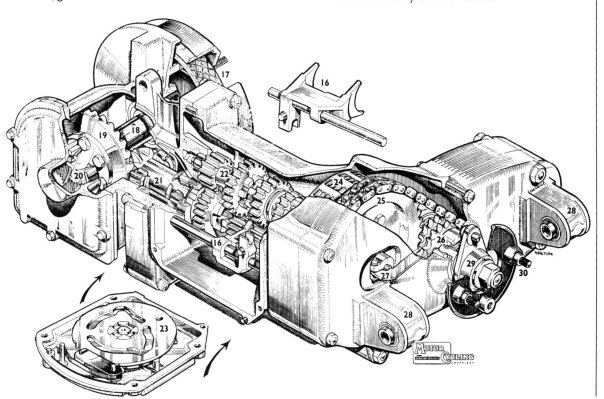

Left **Viceroy crankshaft construction with caged roller big ends and pressed up construction**

Right below **Dashboard of Viceroy with petrol tank filler behind it**

Below **The Viceroy scooter with its heel and toe rocking pedal gearchange**

110

At the rear of the crankshaft went a flywheel and this was cut with gear teeth for a starter. This was a car type electric motor mounted on top of the crankcase to the left side. It was of the pre-engaged type where the operating lever first moved the drive gear into mesh with the flywheel one and then closed the switch contacts. On the Viceroy the lever protruded from the bodywork so operation was very direct.

From the back of the flywheel the power was taken by a short propeller shaft to the transmission. The shaft was simplicity itself being simply a tube with each end split and splayed out for its attachment bolts. At each end it bolted to universal joints comprising a disc with studs in rubber bushes to link to each side.

The transmission was in one unit which contained primary reduction, clutch, gearbox, rear bevel box and rear brake. This unit was built up from light alloy castings and pivoted as an arm from two well-spaced bushes at the front. Its movement was controlled by a single Girling spring and hydraulic damper unit.

Within the transmission were many features from the flat twin machines but also one that was new. This was the primary reduction which was by duplex chain and this carried the drive line from the machine centre out to the right. It then went back via a conventional clutch with four bonded inserts and five plain plates. The input shaft it was attached to ran in a ball race at the front and a needle at the rear while the

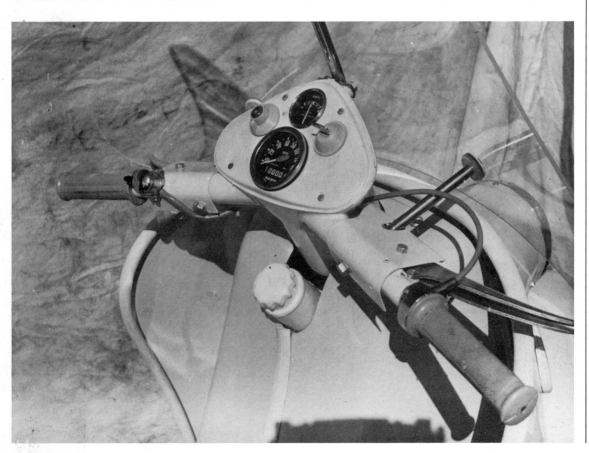

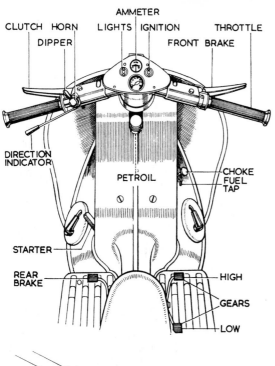

CLUTCH HORN AMMETER LIGHTS IGNITION THROTTLE
DIPPER FRONT BRAKE
DIRECTION INDICATOR
PETROIL
CHOKE FUEL TAP
STARTER
REAR BRAKE
HIGH
GEARS
LOW

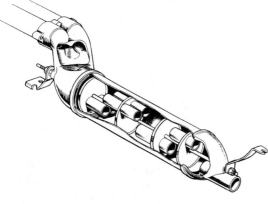

Above **Silencer—to be dismantled before removing rear wheel**

Top **Viceroy control layout**

Viceroy publicity photo which emphasises the large build of the scooter

output below it was the other way round. It also extended back to the rear bevel pinion.

The gearbox contained four speeds and was in essence that of the later LE and Valiant laid on its side. The gears and their selectors were precisely the same and the positive stop mechanism went on the side. Gear changing was by a rocking pedal pivoted on the frame and linked by rod to the mechanism.

At the rear it was the crown wheel and pinion as before with the brake mounted on the inboard side of the housing and the speedometer driven by a gear on the right end of the rear axle.

The frame to which this unconventional engine and transmission was attached to was based on a single massive tube which ran down from the headstock and up again beneath the

A DMW Deemster for the police fitted with a Viceroy engine in place of its normal Villiers twin

seat. Cross tubes and pressing hung down to support the engine unit, provide pivot points for the transmission cum rear suspension arm and to carry the minor details.

The fuel tank went above the engine just behind the headstock and carried 2¼-gallons of petroil mixed at 20:1 for two-stroke oil and a rich 16:1 if the owner used self mix. Lubrication of the rest of the mechanics, primary chain, gearbox and bevel box was by one oil with a single filler located behind a rubber cap.

At the front of the frame went telescopic forks based on LE units while at the rear a single Girling spring and damper unit controlled the move-

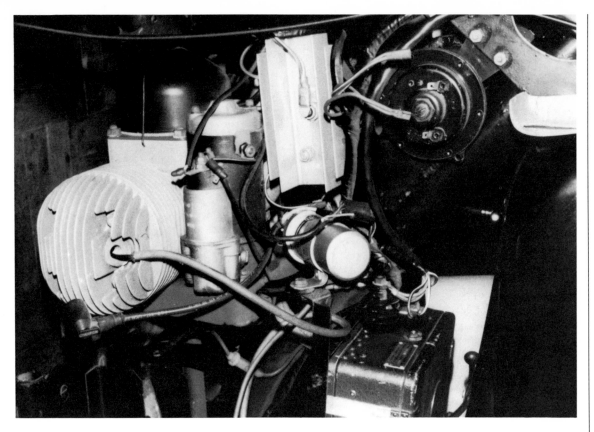

The Viceroy engine installed in the Deemster

ment of the swinging arm assembly. Both wheels were pressed disc types and at 12 in. diameter larger than usual for a scooter. Tyre section was 4 in. and the wheel rims were not split in the normal scooter style.

Each wheel was bolted to its 6 in. diameter brake drum and the front one had a knock out spindle while the rear went on a stub axle. Single leading shoe brakes were fitted and their adjustment was unusual and designed to always leave the cam lever in the optimum position. To achieve this a pinion was locked to the cam spindle with the lever free to turn about it. To connect the two a rack went in the lever and transmitted its force to the pinion and thus the cam. This force went through a face which was a nut and by turning this the cam could be

adjusted while the lever remained static.

At the top of the forks went a light alloy casting onto which was fixed the instrument panel. This had the speedometer in its centre with an ammeter ahead of it and flanked by a light switch on the left and an ignition one to the right. The handlebars were two stubs which were clamped into the casting with covers to conceal the cables and wiring. Included in the controls was a direction indicator switch which went on the left bar along with the horn button and dipper.

The working parts were enclosed by a body which comprised six sections and its job was assisted by a front mudguard blade fitted to the

forks to keep road dirt off the engine. Over it went a front assembly and this comprised the visible and massive front mudguard, headlamp housing and weathershield. This last was formed to accept the windscreen fitted as standard. Behind it went a left and right tank panel each held in place by three Dzus fasteners and to match them were left and right footboards. These bolted to the subframe and also the rear panel assembly and both had rubber foot strips attached to them. The rear assembly was typical of scooters and comprised side panels, dualseat mount and rear mudguard welded into one.

All the panels had access holes of some sort cut in them. There were large round covers to give access to the plugs and the plastic filler cap rose between the tank panels. On the right protruded the choke and fuel tap while the starter was to the left. The rear brake pedal and heel and toe gear pedal were pivoted on the fame but sat above the footboards.

The seat lifted to reveal twin six-volt batteries wired in series and also the tool kit plus tyre pump. The coils went on a frame plate above the engine with the rectifier ahead of the left one while the horn went between the fork stanchions. At the rear the body was painted black to act as a number plate while plastic panels were provided on the mudguard sides at the front for similar duty.

Finish of the Viceroy was red for all body pressings with white piping, gear and brake pedals, instrument casting and handlebar shroud. The dualseat was in grey and pannier and top cases were available as options finished in tartan. A seat cover to match was also listed which was just the right thing for the scooterist and compensated for the unnecessary ammeter.

The Viceroy was listed at £198 and weighed in at 302 lb. The name was perhaps unfortunate and recalled the days of the raj to a generation

Viceroy with propeller which simply bolted on the end of the crankshaft. Used for midget hovercraft built as school projects for a brief period

of buyers who had no real knowledge or interest of such matters. They were into coffee bars and the local social life so the fact the Velocette gave most of their models a name beginning with the letter V was of no import at all.

The machine was also on the large size. Most scooters were light, nimble, Italian, *feminine* and were advertised by blondes in bikinis. On the Viceroy they were dwarfed and this massive appearance put the machine into the teutonic class at once. It also meant a model that was awkward to manage when wheeling it in a parking lot or to get down the side alley of a house.

Reports indicate that it was not smooth when ticking over although very nice once under way. This was all part of the Velocette pattern of doing the job right as to them operational correctness was all. So the Viceroy handled well, had a good performance and the power to cope with hills and headwinds without problems. It was also rather noisy and the starter engaged with odd sounds and all this coupled with doubtful sounding slow running was what the average buyer saw.

Thus with a prejudice against British scooters and no real standards to compare the machine against or with, most customers opted out of a trial run and walked off to the nearest Lambretta or Vespa dealer. To many, scooter meant Italian just as in years to come Honda was to mean motorcycle to so many of the same buying public.

The Viceroy was basically unchanged during its life but during 1961 the choice of colours was increased to include pale blue, willow green and polychromatic green as well as the original red. All came with the white as before and the model continued in this form through 1962.

For 1963 there were some detail changes with an improved air filter, a push-choke rod and a shield over the starter motor to keep it clean. Also the seat was hinged to one side and Ferodo inserts went into the clutch. A curious addition was an air slide in the carburettor which was not connected to a control but went in to reduce turbulence within the instrument. The colours were listed as primrose yellow, powder blue, willow green, deep polychromatic green or red, all with the white as before.

There were a few more changes for 1964 but the finish remained as it was. A chain tensioner was added to the primary transmission and the gearchange linkage was stiffened up to give a better and more positive feel to the movement. Rubber buffers went on the fork lock stops to prevent clashing while there were also changes within the engine.

The first concerned the main bearings which were changed to ball races while the setting for the reed valve tops were altered. On the electrics the alternator low speed output was boosted by

changing the coil tappings and the main switch revised to prevent accidental running on the emergency circuit.

This failed to make much impression on what was by then a dwindling market and although the model was listed for 1965 production of it came to a halt late in 1964. The engine unit was later used in some DMW Deemster models for the police, also modified for midget hovercraft used in the late sixties. This second field was a short lived school project craze and brought Velocette a little more business for a while.

So ended the last new Velocette design, a victim of the Goodman determination to do a proper job in a proper engineering fashion. All rather sad but perhaps an epitaph they could appreciate.

Appendix

1 Specifications

Model	LE	LE MkII	LE MkIII	Vogue
Year from	**1948**	**1950**	**1958**	**1963**
Year to	**1950**	**1958**	**1971**	**1968**
Bore (mm)	44	50	50	50
Stroke (mm)	49	49	49	49
Capacity (cc)	149	192	192	192
Compression ratio (to 1)	6·0	6·0/7·0	7·0	7·0
Valve position	sv	sv	sv	sv
inlet opens BTDC	20	20		
inlet closes ABDC	55	55		
exhaust opens BBDC	55	55		
exhaust closes ATDC	20	20		
Valve clear. (cold) in. (in.)	0·004	0·004	0·004	0·004
Valve clear. (cold) ex. (in.)	0·006	0·006	0·006	0·006
Ignition timing (in.)	0·156	tdc	tdc	tdc
Points gap (in.)	0·012	0·015	0·015	0·015
Box ratio: top		0·739	0·739	0·739
Box ratio: 3rd			1·0	1·0
Box ratio: 2nd		1·105	1·353	1·353
Box ratio: 1st		2·078	2·078	2·078
O/A ratio: top	7·15	7·256	7·256	7·256
O/A ratio: 3rd			9·818	9·818
O/A ratio: 2nd	13·0	10·85	13·28	13·28
O/A ratio: 1st	21·0	20·40	20·40	20·40
Tyres (in.)	3·00 × 19	3·00 × 19 **1**	3·25 × 18	3·25 × 18
Rims	WM1-LA	WM1 **2**	WM2	WM2
Brake dia. (in.)	5	5	5	5
Brake front width (in.)	0·75	0·75 **3**	1·0	1·0
Brake rear width (in.)	0·75	0·75 **4**	1·0	1·0
Front suspension	teles	teles	teles	teles
Rear type	s/a	s/a	s/a	s/a
Petrol tank (Imp. gal)	1·25	1·25 **5**	1·62	2·5
Oil capacity (Imp. pint)	1·25	1·25 **6**	1·75	1·75
Box capacity (Imp. pint)	0·25	0·25	0·25	0·25

Model	LE	LE MkII	LE MkIII	Vogue
Year from	**1948**	**1950**	**1958**	**1963**
Year to	**1950**	**1958**	**1971**	**1968**
Final drive (Imp. pint)	0·25	0·25	0·25	0·25
Ignition system	coil	coil	coil	coil
Generator type	dynamo	dynamo **7**	alt	alt
Output (Watts)	30	42	42 **8**	42 or 80 **8**
Battery (Volt)	6	6	6 **9**	6 **9**
Wheelbase (in.)	51·2	51·2	51·2	51·6
Ground clear. (in.)	5·5	4·5	4·5	4·5
Seat height (in.)	28	28	28	28
Width (bars) (in.)	25			
Length (in.)	82			
Dry weight (lb)	250	250	263	275
Power: bhp	6	8	8	8
@ rpm	5000	5000	5000	5000

1 1956—3·25 × 18   **2** 1956—WM2   **3** 1954—1·0   **4** 1953—1·0   **5** 1955—1·62   **6** 1953—1·75
7 1951—alt for some   **8** 1965—90   **9** 1965—12

Model	Valiant	Vee Line	Viceroy
Year from	**1956**	**1958**	**1960**
Year to	**1964**	**1960**	**1964**
Bore (mm)	50	50	54
Stroke (mm)	49	49	54
Capacity (cc)	192	192	247
Compression ratio (to 1)	8·5 **1**	8·0 **2**	7·5
Valve position	ohv	ohv	reed
inlet opens BTDC	40	40	
inlet closes ABDC	60	60	
exhaust open BBDC	60	60	
exhaust closes ATDC	40	40	
Valve clear. (cold) in. (in.)	0·004	0·004	
Valve clear. (cold) ex. (in.)	0·006	0·006	
Ignition timing degree	42	42	
Points gap (in.)	0·015	0·015	0·105
Sprockets: engine (T)			19
Sprockets: clutch (T)			43
Box ratio: top	0·739	0·739	0·739
Box ratio: 3rd	1·0	1·0	1·0
Box ratio: 2nd	1·353	1·353	1·353
Box ratio: 1st	2·078	2·078	2·078
O/A ratio: top	7·256	7·256	5·02
O/A ratio: 3rd	9·818	9·818	6·79
O/A ratio: 2nd	13·28	13·28	9·19
O/A ratio: 1st	20·40	20·40	14·1

Model	Valiant	Vee Line	Viceroy
Year from	1956	1958	1960
Year to	1964	1960	1964
Tyres (in.)	3·25 × 18	3·25 × 18	4·00 × 12
Rims	WM2	WM2	pressed
Brake dia. (in.)	5	5	6
Brake width (in.)	1	1	1
Front suspension	teles	teles	teles
Rear type	s/a	s/a	s/a
Petrol tank (Imp. gal)	3·0	3·0	2·25
Oil capacity (Imp. pint)	1·75	1·75	
Box capacity (Imp. pint)	0·25	0·25	1·5
Final drive (Imp. pint)	0·25	0·25	
Ignition system	coil	coil	coil
Generator type	alt	alt	alt
Output (Watts)	42	42	60
Battery (Volt)	6	6	12
Wheelbase (in.)	51·2	51·2	53
Ground clear. (in.)	6	6	5
Seat height (in.)	29	29	29
Length (in.)			79
Dry weight (lb)	255	276	302
Power: bhp	12	12	
@ rpm	6000 **3**	7000	

1 1957—8·0, 1960—7·8, 1961—7·0 **2** 1960—7·8 **3** 1958—7000

2 Colours

LE

1949–50

Main frame pressing, top and bottom fork crown, front mudguard, front fork legs, front fork lower shrouds and saddle bracket in silver grey. Polished alloy legshields and wheel rims, chrome plated fork stanchions and headlamp rim, dull chrome-plated exhaust pipes. Black headlamp shell, handlebars, headstock, radiator surround, rear engine pressing, rear fork, footboards, cylinders, sump, hubs, generator, silencer box, number plates, battery strap, stand, rear brake pedal and pannier frames. Also saddle top and pillion black and black footboard rubbers.

1951–54

As 1949–50 except headlamp shell in silver grey.

1955

Two-tone options added. Colour of ruby, green or pale blue applied to front mudguard, rear mudguard section of main frame and lower edge of main frame. Black separating line. Chrome plated embellishing strips along lower frame edge, plated trim from rear pivot area to edge of rear mudguard and chrome plated wheel rims. During year alloy rear fork adopted in natural cast conditon.

1956

Addition of dove grey as two-tone option colour and legshields painted to match mudguards.

1957

Addition of polychromatic olive green as two-tone option colour. Chrome plated handlebars.

1958–59

Standard finish as 1949 except chrome-plated wheel rims and handlebars. Two-tone options as 1955 with second colour willow or light green, polychromatic or deep green, or blue.

MkIII as MkII but legshields always silver grey so two-tone finish applied to mudguards and lower body edge only. Legshield tops polished alloy.

1960–66

Handlebars in silver grey.

1967–71

Basic colour given as light grey, police models in black and two-tone options as 1958.

Valiant

1957–58

Dark green or black frame, forks, tank, headlamp shell, mudguards, toolbox, engine cowl. Petrol tank with gold lining. Chrome plated rear lifting stays, exhaust pipes, silencers, wheel rims, headlamp rim, handlebars and tank holding down strap. Chrome-plated options were crash bars and tank side panels.

1959

As 1957, Vee Line fairing to match machine colour.

1960–64

Colours given as black or willow green.

Vogue

1963

Porcelain white body, front mudguard and forks. Rich stone side panels, legshields and panniers. Dualseat fawn with brown sides and cross panel. Mechanics as for LE with alternator cover in white. Chrome-plated exhaust pipes, handlebars, wheel rims and headlamp rims.

1964

As 1963 in off white and stone.

1965–66

As 1963 in ivory and stone.

1967–68

As 1963 in white and grey.

Viceroy

1961

Pannelling red with white piping and white wheels, steering head casting, instrument panel, handlebar shrouds and front fork. Grey seat, tartan panniers and seat cover option. During year alternative's in pale blue, willow green or polychromatic green with white.

1962

As 1961.

1963–64

As 1961 in primrose yellow, powder blue, willow green, deep polychromatic green or red with white.

---

3 Engine and frame numbers

On the first LE models the engine number was stamped on the machined surface of the crankcase beneath the carburettor. The frame number was on a plate inside the toolbox lid. Around 1955 the engine number was included on the toolbox lid plate but continued to be stamped on the crankcase as well. On the MkIII model the engine number was moved to the crankcase area behind the carburettor.

The Vogue had the same engine number location while the frame number was stamped on the flat plate of the vertical centre frame member on the right side of the machine.

The Valiant began with its engine number stamped on top of the crankcase but from 1958 it was moved to the right side of the crankcase ahead of the cylinder barrel. The frame number went on the left-hand side rear suspension bracket.

LE

Year	Model	Engine	Frame	Feature
1948	MkI	1001	1001	
1950		6374	6393	
last		c.8500	c.8500	
1951	MkII	200/10001	8500	
		200/11324	9851	lubrication system change

Year	Model	Engine	Frame	Feature
6/1951		200/12640	11179	Miller AC3
1/1952		200/15840	14378	Miller AC3P
5/1953		200/18975	17523	3 plate clutch
		200/19393	17917	1 in.wide rear brake
7/1953		200/19609	18154	external oil filter
8/1953		200/19917	18456	plain bearing crankshaft
10/1953		200/20253	18773	Miller AC4 only
11/1953		200/20344	18878	radiator frame modification
1954		200/20992	19521	1 in. wide front brake
7/1954		200/21331	19860	modified battery box
2/1955		200/22637	21550	plain bearing camshaft
2/1955		200/22678	21190	wider big ends
5/1955		200/23526	20246	cast alloy rear fork
10/1955				larger fuel tank
11/1955		200/24339	22956	chrome top ring
10/1956		200/25503	23967	Monobloc carburettor
10/1956		200/25527	24019	deeper oil sump
10/1956		200/25539	24081	18 in. rims, full width hubs
1957		200/26083	24689	MkII continued
1958		200/27264	25758	MkII continued
last		200/27395	25884	last MkII
1958	MkIII	1001/3	1001/34	
1959		1954/3	1954/34	
2/1959		2166/3	2166/34	piston ring modification
1960		2992/3	2992/34	
1961		3958/3	3958/34	
1962		4681/3	4681/34	
9/1962		5071/3	5095/34	
1963		5271/3	5271/34	
1964		5985/3	5985/34	
1964		6533/3	6533/34	Lucas electrics modified engine, 12 volts
1965		6800/3	6800/34	
1966		7523/3	7523/34	
1967		8030/3	8030/34	stiffer body
1968		8592/3	8592/34	
1969		8720/3	8720/34	
1970		8962/3	8962/34	
2/1971		9071/3	9071/34	last MkIII

Valiant

Year	Engine	Frame
11/1956	V200/1001	1001/33
3/1958	V200/1208	1217/33
11/1958	V200/1888	1988/33
1959	V200/2211	2304/33
1960	V200/2290	2426/33
1961	V200/2454	2468/33
1962	V200/2565	2552/33
1963	V200/2581	2321/33
Mid-1963	V200/2601	2344/33

*Note out of sequence—possibly caused by slow sales

Vogue

Year	Engine	Frame
2/1963	5606/3	101/37
1964	5982/3	199/37
1965	6800/3	345/37
1966	7523/3	434/37
1967	8025/3	457/37
1968	8592/3	476/37
3/1968	8651/3	481/37*

*Last of 381 machines

Viceroy

Year	Engine	Frame
1961	SE 101	S 101
1962	SE 579	S 625
9/1962	SE 605	S 660
1964	SE 773	S 755
last	SE 798	S 782

DMW Deemster engines SE 888 to SE 925. Hovercraft engines—up to SE 1164

4 Carburettor settings

Fixed jet type

Model	Year	Main jet	Starter jet	Pilot jet	Compensating jet	Spray tubes	Pilot spray tube
LE150	1948–50	20	15	30	25	145	25
LE200	1951–53	25	15	30	25	145	25
LE200	1954–56	25	15	25	20	145	20

Slide type

Model	Year	Type	Size	Main jet	Pilot jet	Slide	Needle pos.	Needle jet
LE	1956–58	363/1	·475	65	25	2	3	·1045
LE and Vogue	1959–64	363/7	·475	65	25	2	3	·104
LE and Vogue	1965–71	19/5	.5	95	15	2	3	·104
Valiant	1957–64	363/4 & 5	·625	100	15	2	3	·104
Viceroy	1961–64	376/259	1.062	210	25	3	3	·105

5 Prices

The UK prices of the machines are set out in the tables next and include the purchase tax that was payable on them. Certain accessories were exempt from this. Many of the price changes in the early 1950s were due to tax changes rather than makers while the basic cost varied little.

Date	LE	Valiant	Vee Line
28.10.48	£126. 7s. 4d.		
15. 9.49	£148. 6s. 9d.		
9.11.50	£158.15s. 0d.		
12. 7.51	£168.18s. 3d.		
11.10.51	£169.18s.11d.		
30.10.52	£173.15s. 7d.		
29.10.53	£163. 4s. 0d.		
20.10.55	£167. 8s. 0d.		
4.10.56	£182.18s. 0d.		
1.11.56		£181.13s. 2d.	
29. 8.57		£199.12s.10d.	
5. 9.57	£193. 7s. 3d.	£200.16s.11d.	
9. 1.58	£202.14s. 5d.		
11. 9.58		£217. 1s. 4d.	£238.17s.11d.
3. 9.59	£196. 0s. 4d.	£209.17s. 9d.	£230.19s.11d.
13.10.60		£215. 0s. 0d.	

Date	LE	Valiant	Vogue	Viceroy
3.11.60				£198. 0s. 0d.
14. 9.61	£209.10s. 5d.	£208.15s. 0d.		£201. 7s. 8d.
20. 9.62	£217. 4s. 6d.	£216. 8s. 8d.		£208.15s.10d.
15.11.62			£239.19s. 9d.	
26. 9.63	£217. 4s. 6d.	£216. 8s. 8d.	£239.19s. 9d.	£175. 0s. 0d.
18. 7.64			£246. 0s. 0d.	
15.10.64	£235. 4s. 0d.			£189.12s. 0d.
11. 9.65	£240. 9s. 7d.		£252. 3s. 0d.	
27.10.66	£253. 1s. 0d.		£269. 6s. 3d.	

LE options

Date	Two-tone	Dualseat	Panniers	Steel panniers	Luggage grid	Screen
4.11.54	£3.18s. 0d.	£3.15s. 7d.				
20.10.55	£2.14s. 0d.	£2.11s. 7d.	£3. 2s.11d.			
4.10.56	£4. 0s. 7d.	£3.18s. 2d.	£3. 5s. 0d.	£8.15s. 0d.	£2. 1s. 9d.	
9. 1.58	£4. 1s. 1d.	£3.18s. 7d.				
11. 9.58			£3. 5s. 5d.	£8.15s. 0d.	£2. 1s. 9d.	£6. 5s. 0d.
3. 9.59	£3.18s. 5d.	£3.16s. 0d.	£3. 3s 3d.	£8.15s. 0d.	£2. 1s. 9d.	£6.15s. 0d.
13.10.60						£5.19s. 6d.
14. 9.61	£3.19s. 9d.	£3.17s. 4d.	£3. 4s. 4d.		£2. 1s. 9d.	£5.19s. 6d.
27.10.66	£4.18s. 4d.					

Date	Pedal conversion	Oil gauge	Petrol can	Stop light	13 amp batteries	12-volt battery
4.10.56	£1. 6s. 8d.					
11. 9.58		£2.19s. 6d.				
3. 9.59		£2.19s. 6d.	£1. 5s. 0d.			
13.10.60				12s.11d.		
14. 9.61		£2.19s. 6d.	£1. 5s. 0d.	12s. 3d.		
15.10.64					£1.12s.10d.	£3. 9s. 3d.

Valiant options

Date	Crash bars	Pillion rests	Stop light	Chrome tank panels	Left toolbox	Pannier set
29. 8.57	£3.10s. 0d.	£1.11s. 6d.	12s. 5d.	£2.15s.10d.	£1.17s. 2d.	
11. 9.58			14s. 4d.	£2.16s. 2d.	£1.17s. 5d.	£6.14s. 4d.
3. 9.59			12s. 1d.	£2.14s. 4d.	£1.16s. 2d.	£6.12s.10d.
13.10.60			13s.11d.			
14. 9.61	£3.10s. 0d.	£1.11s. 6d.	14s. 2d.	£2.15s. 3d.	£1.16s. 9d.	£6.13s. 7d.

Vogue options
at 18.7.64

Panniers	£13.13s. 0d.
Winkers	£7. 1s. 7d.
Screen	£5.15s. 0d.
Carrier	£3. 1s. 0d.
Stop light	15s. 7d.

Viceroy options
at 3.11.60

Screen	£5. 0s. 0d.
Enamelled carrier	£5. 5s. 0d.
Chromed carrier	£7.15s. 0d.
Octopus elastic	8s. 0d.
Top case and panniers	£7.12s. 6d.
Tartan seat cover	£1. 7s. 6d.

6 Model recognition

These notes are to some extent a precis of the main text and should be used in conjunction with it and the other appendices.

LE

1949

Original 149 cc model with hand change, hand starter, panniers, BTH generator and petrol tap screwed into carburettor.

1951

192 cc model, same exterior, new crankshaft, tappets, increased oil delivery, gudgeon pin retained by circlips, raised second gear, stronger clutch springs, revised oil system, Hookes joint for final drive shaft, some machines with Miller AC3 generator, some machines with ball bearing head races.

1952

Miller AC3P generator.

1953

Plain mains and big ends, pressure oil feed, external oil filter mounted on right cylinder head, third clutch plate, no link between stand and hand start lever, access hole in left side of main frame, 1 in. wide rear brake shoes, modified tubular frame to aid servicing.

1954

No access hole in left side of main frame, modified battery carrier, 1 in. wide front brake shoes, no BTH generator, Miller AC4 generator, new rectifier position.

1955

Plain camshaft bearings with oilways to suit, wider big end bearings, moulded lower hoses, induction pipe heater using top hose connections, chrome trim added to lower edges of main frame, separate rear number plate support, bolted on pillion seat bracket. Option of two level dualseat and two-tone finish. In middle of year light alloy rear fork adopted.

1956

Increased petrol capacity, taper face chrome plated top piston rings, panniers became an extra, metal streamlined panniers added to option list. Late in year tyres changed to 3·25 × 18 in., full width hubs, 363 Amal Monobloc carburettor, intake oil filter mounted on oil pump, sump without filter access hole, petrol tap hole in left side of main frame.

1957

Further options of oil pressure gauge, right side rear brake pedal and petrol can with mounting bracket.

1958

MkIII model introduced with four speeds, Valiant bottom half, footchange, kickstarter, no induction heater, gearbox rear plate held by four bolts, speedometer drive from left front corner of gearbox, silencer indented to accommodate gearbox, petrol tap hole in right side of main frame, shrouded forks, headlamp cowl, switch and instruments in headlamp shell, revised handlebars, horn set in right legshield, licence holder mounted on front of left legshield, no licence holder incorporated in front number plate which became of regular form. Saddle fitted as

standard, option of dualseat and option of oil pressure gauge fitted into left legshield top.
Three-speed model continued as MkII but discontinued late in year.

1959
Piston rings modified, windscreen option added.

1961
Headlamp rims modified. Stop lamp option added but metal pannier option no longer listed.

1964
During year change to Lucas electrics.

1965
12-volt electrics by Lucas, zener diode mounted on underside of toolbox, switches and ammeter in right legshield top panel, speedometer only in headlamp shell, twin batteries or option of single 12-volt unit, heavier gauge main frame beam, heavier rear brake pedal with toe guard, wider timing gears, increased oil feed to crankshaft, revised coolant passages, waisted propeller shaft, larger crown wheel and pinion, type 19 carburettor.

1967
Stiffening added to main frame beam.

1971
End of production in February.

Valiant

1957
Orthodox motorcycle with air cooled, flat twin engine, four-speed gearbox, duplex frame, LE forks and pivoted rear fork, LE wheels, cowl over engine unit, toolbox on right as standard with option of left one, Woodhead-Munroe rear units and blade mudguards. Early in year changed to Girling rear units, valanced rear mudguards with revised lifting handles, lowered compression ratio and improved silencers.

1958
Balance pipe between inlet stubs added, engine number position moved to right crankcase ahead of barrel, option of panniers added.

1959
Vee Line model offered with dolphin fairing and fitted as standard with chrome-plated tank side panels.

1960
7·8:1 compression ratio, Vee Line model dropped in October.

1961
No changes announced but during year brackets added on frame for exhaust pipes, compression ratio became 7·0:1 two gaskets fitted under each cylinder, washer fitted between each tappet and its screwed in pin.

1962–63
No changes.

1964
End of production in August.

Vogue

1963
LE mechanics fitted to tubular spine frame with fibreglass bodywork. Twin headlights, legshields, indicators. Indicator lever in instrument panel, Miller 42 watt generator.

1964
80 watt Miller generator, indicator lever on right handlebar.

1965
Engine and transmission modified as for LE, type 19 carburettor, still six-volt electrics.

1966
12-volt Lucas electrics.

1968
End of production.

Viceroy

1961
Scooter with 250 cc flat twin two-stroke engine, 12 in. wheels.

1963
Improved air filter, push-pull choke rod, starter motor shield, seat hinged to one side, Ferodo clutch inserts, air slide fitted to carburettor but not connected.

1964

Chain tensioner added, stiffened gearchange link, fork lock
stop buffers, ball race mains, reed valve settings altered,
alternator tappings revised, main switch improved.
End of production late in year.

7 Model chart

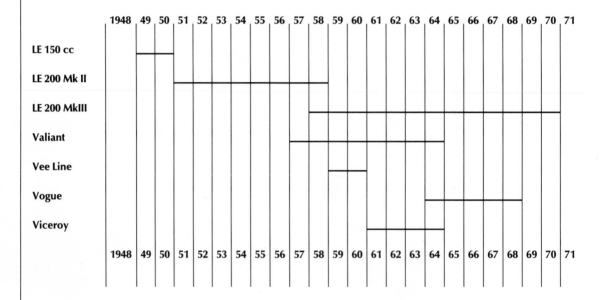